Practical
Pre-School

What ...g Lou... Like...

Language
and Literacy

Hilary White

Contents

What Learning *Looks Like...*

Language
and **Literacy**

About this book

This book takes a close look at one of the six areas of learning in the curriculum guidelines across the United Kingdom - Language and Literacy in England and Wales, Communication and Language in Scotland and Language Development in Northern Ireland.

Guidance and good practice

The author explains what the area of learning consists of, what the jargon means and how it applies to the various settings in the Foundation Stage of education - children aged between three and rising six.

There are four different curriculum bodies across the United Kingdom - the Qualifications and Curriculum Authority (QCA) in England; the Curriculum and Assessment Authority for Wales (Awdurdod Cwricwlwm Ac Asesu Cymru); the Scottish Consultative Council on the Curriculum; and the Northern Ireland Council for the Curriculum Examinations and Assessment. Each has a different statement relating to the desired curriculum for young children. However, although there are some differences in terminology and some slight variations in emphasis, good practice in one country is still considered good practice in another. The text includes references throughout to the different systems which allows early years practitioners to put the correct terms in their planning and for inspection purposes.

As well as giving theoretical guidance - albeit in practical terms - the book also offers suggestions for activities which

can be used to deliver the curriculum requirements.

Practical activities

All these activities should be considered as merging into the normal life of the early years setting. We have stressed the importance of play and how the different areas of learning are linked. The activities are not prescriptive and should not be seen as tasks to complete. They are designed to be manageable and fun.

There are suggestions for 15 activities. Some are simple and straightforward activities which need few resources. Others are deliberately more challenging. Each can be used in some form with children at different stages of development.

There can be no prescriptive 'at four-and-a-half a child should be able to ...' and although children tend to move along a continuum of development their progress will not necessarily be steady or uniform. Any age-related guidance should be seen as what it is meant to be - for guidance only.

If followed throughout the year the activities cover all the Language and Literacy Early Learning Goals (ELGs). Many of the ELGs overlap and interrelate with one another. The activities therefore often fulfil more than one ELG. All the activities follow the same format. Ideas for assessment are also included.

The books have been designed to be suitable for all types of settings from

school reception classroom to church hall. You may want to adapt and change them to make them more appropriate for the group of children you are teaching. If used in conjunction with the *Planning for Learning* series, also from Step Forward Publishing, they should provide a basis for planned work in all aspects of the Foundation Stage of education.

Planning

A planning chart has been included for support and guidance but we would encourage our readers to adapt this readily to their own needs and circumstances.

There are seven books in this series, and although each book can be used by itself, they are designed to fit together so that the whole learning framework is covered.

The seven titles are:

❏ Language and Literacy

❏ Creative Development

❏ Mathematical Development

❏ Personal, Social and Emotional Development

❏ Physical Development

❏ Knowledge and Understanding of the World: Geography and History

❏ Knowledge and Understanding of the World: Science and Technology.

All of these books carry some activities based on common themes which, when used together, will give enough ideas for a cross-curriculum topic over a half or even a full term.

The common themes are:

❑ Seasons

❑ Water

❑ Colour

❑ All about me

❑ People who help us

All the books together provide an outline of the learning which should be taking place in the Foundation Stage.

Assessment

Each activity includes an assessment section. Assessment involves two distinct activities:

❑ The gathering of information about the child's capabilities.

❑ Making a judgement based on this information.

Assessment should not take place in isolation. We assess to meet individual needs and ensure progress. The following ideas may help your assessment to be more effective.

❑ Assessment is a continuous process. It should be systematic to ensure all children are observed on a regular basis.

❑ Assessment should always start with the child. The first steps in providing appropriate provision is by sensitively observing children to identify their learning needs.

❑ Assessment should not take place to see how much the child has learned but should take place to plan appropriately for future activities.

❑ You should be a participant in the assessment process, interacting and communicating with the child.

The main way of assessing the young child is through careful observation.

Observations should:

❑ Record both the positive and negative behaviour shown.

❑ Be long enough to make the child's behaviour meaningful.

❑ Record only what you see and not what you think you have seen or heard.

❑ Be clear - before you begin be sure you know what you want to observe.

❑ Be organised - plan ahead, otherwise it will not happen.

National guidelines

The English Early Learning Goals

The Early Learning Goals were published in October 1999. They set out what most children are expected to achieve by the end of the Foundation Stage.

The Foundation Stage runs from the age of three to the end of the reception year (the first year of compulsory schooling.) The child's age at the end of reception can vary considerably, from 5.0 in the case of an August birthday to 5.11 if the child was born in September. This should be taken into account when assessing whether or not a child should have reached a goal by the end of reception. Because the Early Learning Goals are aimed at the child who is rising six, most pre-school settings will be working towards them, rather than expecting children in their care to achieve them.

Although the goals are not a curriculum in themselves, they cover the six curricular areas of Personal, Social and Emotional Development, Language and Literacy, Mathematical Development, Knowledge and Understanding of the World, Creative Development and Physical Development.

The Language and Literacy section of the Early Learning Goals document includes a list of the learning opportunities the early years worker should plan for, the Early Learning Goals themselves and illustrative examples of children engaged in typical activities and how these relate to certain goals.

The Early Learning Goals for Language and Literacy are in line with the objectives set out in the National Literacy Strategy. Although the goals are presented as a single list, it is possible to put them into broad categories relating either to speaking/listening skills, reading or writing. It is, however, important to remember that the child's development in one area of language and literacy feeds into her development in others. Many of the goals reflect this in having a significance for all aspects of language and literacy.

Speaking and listening

The various branches include:

❑ the social purpose of communication in 'interact with others, negotiating plans and activities and taking turns in conversation' and 'speak clearly and audibly with confidence and control and show awareness of the listener ...';

❑ the organisational potential of language in 'use talk to organise, sequence and clarify thinking, ideas, feelings and events';

❑ the creative potential of language in 'use language to imagine and recreate roles and experiences'.

Two of the goals relate particularly to listening skills, stating that the child should be able to:

❑ 'sustain attentive listening ...'

❑ 'listen with enjoyment ... to stories, songs and other music, rhymes and poems'.

Enjoying language and stories

The theme of enjoyment, the creative possibilities of language and the importance of stories, poems and rhymes can be found in a number of the goals. For example, children should be able to:

❑ 'enjoy listening to and using spoken and written language, and readily turn to it in their play and learning';

❑ 'explore and experiment with sounds, words and texts';

❑ 'make up their own stories, songs, rhymes and poems'.

The goal to 'make up their own stories, songs, rhymes and poems' is expanded upon later in the list with the more formal and specific goals requiring the child to 'retell narratives in the correct sequence, drawing on the language patterns of stories' and 'extend their vocabulary, exploring the meanings and sounds of new words'.

Reading and writing

All of the goals contribute to and prepare for the development of reading and writing skills, but there are certain goals that link specifically with reading and writing. Some of these prepare for both writing and reading. For example, children should be able to:

❑ 'hear and say initial and final sounds in words, and short vowel sounds within words';

❑ 'link sounds to letters, naming and sounding the letters of the alphabet';

❑ 'know that print carries meaning and, in English, is read from left to right and top to bottom'.

Some of the goals relate more closely to reading and cover the different strands that make up whole reading. For example:

❑ the beginnings of actual reading in 'read a range of familiar and common words and, simple sentences independently';

❑ reading for meaning in 'show an understanding of the elements of stories, such as main character, sequence of events, and openings, and how information can be found in non-fiction texts to answer questions about where, who, why and how'.

Other goals have a more obvious link with writing and, as with reading, cover the different branches of writing:

❑ the beginnings of actual writing in 'use their phonic knowledge to write simple, regular words and make phonetically plausible attempts at more complex words';

❑ the content and form of writing in 'attempt writing for various purposes, using features of different forms such as lists, stories and instructions'; and 'write their own names and other things such as labels and captions and begin to form simple sentences, sometimes using punctuation';

❑ the physical element of writing in 'use a pencil and hold it effectively to form recognisable letters, most of which are correctly formed'.

Although the goals are loosely organised into the three areas of speaking and listening, reading and writing, the order in which they are listed is not always logical. For example, 'read a range of familiar and common words and simple sentences independently' comes earlier in the list than 'know that print carries meaning

and, in English, is read from left to right and top to bottom' even though knowledge that English is read from left to right is prerequisite to reading sentences. It is also worth bearing in mind that the goals range from the general, such as 'sustain attentive listening...', to the highly specific, such as 'naming and sounding the letters of the alphabet'. This means that some of the goals overlap in places, with the result that each goal should be considered both singly and as part of the overall pattern of language and literacy development

The Scottish Curriculum Framework

The Scottish Curriculum Framework uses the title Communication and Language for its language and literacy area of learning. Like the English Early Learning Goals, it covers the three broad areas of speaking and listening, early reading and early writing skills.

The major difference between the Scottish and the English advice lies in the age specifications. The Scottish Framework is aimed at children from three to five, whereas the Early Learning Goals focus on what most children should have achieved by the end of the reception year. This makes the Scottish guidance more fluid and much of the advice is general rather than specific: for example, 'children should learn to have fun with language and making stories,' in contrast with the Early Learning Goal of 'retell(ing) narratives in the correct sequence, drawing on the language pattern of stories'.

Listening and speaking

All branches of listening are covered by the Scottish Framework:

❑ listening to other children and adults;

❑ paying attention to 'information and instructions from an adult';

❑ listening and responding to the sounds and rhythm of words in stories, songs, music and rhymes.

A clear emphasis is placed on play and having fun. It is suggested that listening to others should take place during 'social activities and play' and that stories and poems should be listened to 'with enjoyment' and 'enthusiasm'.

'Oral communication' is used for a wide range of purposes and this is recognised in the number of proposed opportunities for talk:

❑ using talk during role-play and retelling a story or rhyme;

❑ expressing 'needs, thoughts and feelings with increasing confidence in talk';

❑ taking part in 'short and more extended conversations'.

❑ using language for a variety of purposes, for example to 'describe, explain, predict, ask questions and develop ideas'.

The Scottish Framework refers to the advantages of exposing children to more than one language - Gaelic, community languages and other European languages are mentioned. It also says that the child's home language should be valued and encouraged.

Reading and writing skills

Although the title Communication and Language does not refer specifically to reading or writing, a wide range of literacy-related skills and experiences are covered in the Scottish Framework. Three of the guidelines relate in particular to the child becoming familiar and comfortable with books:

❑ learning to 'understand some of the language and layout of books';

❑ 'us(ing) books to find interesting information';

❑ 'listen with enjoyment and respond to stories....'.

The mechanics of reading and writing are catered for through learning to:

❑ 'listen and respond to the sounds and rhythms of words in stories, music and rhymes';

❑ 'recognise the link between the written and spoken word' and 'develop an awareness of letter names and sounds'.

The Scottish Framework adds that these learning experiences should take place within the context of play. The English goals are more prescriptive in stating that the child should be able to name and sound 'all the letters of the alphabet' by the end of the reception year.

The most advanced of the reading-related Scottish guidelines states that the child should develop the ability to:

❑ 'recognise some familiar words and letters eg the initial letter in their name' during the pre-school years.

This is a little less extensive and challenging than the parallel English goal of 'read(ing) a range of familiar and common words and simple sentences independently' by the end of the reception year.

The Scottish guidance related to writing focuses on:

❑ 'using their own drawings and written marks to express ideas and feelings';

❑ experimenting with 'symbols, letters, and in some cases, words in writing'.

Both of these guidelines are less technical than the English goal, which specifies that the child should be able to 'form recognisable letters', write 'simple regular words', use phonic knowledge to 'make phonetically plausible attempts at more complex words' and even create sentences.

It is, however, important to reiterate that the Scottish Framework is designed for the pre-school stage whereas the English goals extend to the end of the first year of compulsory schooling.

The Northern Ireland Curricular Guidance for Pre-school Education

The Northern Ireland Curricular Guidance for Pre-School Education uses the title Language Development to describe this area of learning.

The guidance is divided into three sections: a brief overview of the learning area; the learning opportunities that allow for and encourage language development and a general description of the skills and characteristics that the majority of children will display, following appropriate pre-school education.

The list of learning opportunities that help language development include:

❑ 'a wide variety of play activities';

❑ the availability of adults to 'listen to and talk with the children';

❑ 'opportunities to listen to stories, share books with each other and engage in role play';

❑ 'access to a well-stocked library of story and information books';

❑ encouragement to become 'aware of print in the environment';

❑ 'access to a wide variety of painting and drawing materials'.

The characteristics and skills that children display as an indication of progress include:

❑ 'the development of listening and conversational skills' and 'a growing vocabulary';

❑ the ability to 'express thoughts,

ideas and feelings with increasing confidence and fluency' and 'talk about their experiences, ask questions and follow directions and instructions';

❑ the ability to 'listen and respond to stories, nursery rhymes, poems, jingles and songs';

❑ the enjoyment of books and knowledge of 'how to handle them carefully and appropriately';

❑ awareness 'that the printed word has meaning and that it should be read from left to right';

❑ 'creating pictures to convey thoughts or feelings';

❑ 'experiment using symbols' and making 'early attempts at writing'.

Unlike the English goals, these characteristics and skills are not separated under the headings of speaking and listening, reading or writing, although they are divided into three distinct paragraphs. The Northern Ireland guidance also differs from the English goals in advising that 'children should not be introduced to the formal teaching of reading and writing'. As a consequence, no reference is made to the development of phonemic (sound) awareness, beyond stating that the child should have the opportunity to listen to rhymes and jingles. Learning to link sounds and letters is also not mentioned, other than an implicit reference through the writing related guideline that children should be able to 'experiment using symbols . . . and engage in early attempts at writing'. In contrast, the English goals are more prescriptive in stating that children should be able to 'hear and say initial and final sounds in words and short vowel sounds within words'.

Other reading related skills are covered in broad terms: for example, learning that 'the printed word has meaning' as opposed to the specific Early Learning Goal of 'read(ing) a range of familiar and common words and simple sentences'. It is, however, important to remember that the English goal is intended for the child at the end of the reception year, rather than the pre-school stage.

Like the Scottish Curriculum Framework, the Northern Ireland guidance places great emphasis on enjoyment and play experiences. Reference is made to the importance of adults being 'available' to the children and that conversations should take place in a 'relaxed atmosphere'.

The guidelines are also unique in stating that stories should be read to the child in a one-to-one situation as well as in small and large groups.

The Welsh Desirable Outcomes for Children's Learning before Compulsory School Age

The Welsh Desirable Outcomes use the comprehensive title of Language, Literacy and Communication Skills to describe this area of learning.

All branches of language development are covered although the statements are quite brief in comparison with England, Scotland and, to some extent, Northern Ireland. The introductory paragraph to the list of Desirable Outcomes specifies that they should be achieved 'by the age of five'. This is in contrast with the English Early Learning Goals which continue to the end of reception.

Like the Scottish Framework, the Welsh guidance reflects the interdependency of oral language, reading and writing by presenting the outcomes as a single list rather than separating them into three sections. In spite of this, each outcome can be broadly linked with one of the three areas.

Listening and speaking

There are three listening related outcomes:

❑ 'listen to a good story';

❑ 'listen to .... songs, nursery rhymes, poems and jingles';

❑ 'ask questions and listen to responses'.

They differ from the English Early Learning Goals in differentiating between listening situations. Whereas the English goal simply states that children should be able to 'sustain attentive listening', the Welsh Outcomes (like Scotland and Northern Ireland) draw a distinction between listening to stories, poems and rhymes and listening to conversational responses.

A number of the outcomes relate in particular to oral language and communication:

❑ 'communicating needs';

❑ retelling experiences 'broadly in the order in which they occurred';

❑ discussing play and 'referring to intentions';

❑ 'expressing opinions and making choices'.

Literacy

Literacy related outcomes include being able to:

❑ 'relate the broad thrust of a story';

❑ 'identify and explain events illustrated in pictures';

❑ 'choose a book and hold it the right way up'.

As an early form of interpreting symbolic representation, being able to 'read' pictures is a valuable precursor to reading the printed word. The Welsh Desirable Outcomes are alone in making specific reference to this important skill.

The suggestion that the child should be able to choose a book and hold it the right way up is limited in comparison with the English goal, which aims for children to show an understanding of the various story elements, such as the main character. Even though the English goal is aimed at children of up to a year further on in their development and learning, there is quite a gap between these two aims.

The more mechanical elements of reading and writing are covered in general terms. The child should:

❑ 'understand that written symbols have sound and meaning';

❑ 'understand some of the functions of writing';

❑ 'enjoy marking and basic writing experiences'.

Realising that 'written symbols have sound and meaning' is essential, both to reading and writing. As such, this is a broad outcome, with no specification that the child should learn to link symbols with their sounds or use written letters as part of their mark making and early writing experiences. This differs from the much more prescriptive English goal, which states that the child should be able to name and sound the letters of the alphabet by the end of reception. There is also no specification as to what 'basic writing experiences' might consist of, unlike the English goal which is specific in its recommendation that the child should be writing simple words, making attempts at writing more complex words and even forming sentences.

The area of learning explained

Speaking and listening

Language and literacy underpin all aspects of a child's life - her relationships with others, learning about the world, her inner life of thoughts and imaginings to name just three.

The Early Learning Goals divide Language and Literacy into the three broad areas of speaking and listening, reading and writing. Although these divisions are useful when it comes to planning activities for your group, it is important to remember that all three areas overlap. As the child is developing in one area, so her growing skills and capabilities will support the development of the other two.

Beginning conversations

One of the first things to recognise is that the child is constantly developing her language skills, simply by being with you, listening to you and conversing with you. Although there are many wonderful language and literacy based activities that you can do with the children, the planned activity is only a part of the child's learning. The more the child is surrounded by natural, spontaneous conversation, the more she will develop and broaden her skills.

It is not always easy to find time to converse with the children as much as

you might like. Nevertheless, it is important simply to stop, listen and chat. Children soak up a huge amount of general knowledge from conversation with adults. The conversations that take place on the spur of the moment are particularly valuable because they pick up on the child's interests. Whether you are making initial links with the youngest child in your group, or engaging in extensive and complex discussion with a five-year-old, these spontaneous chats will help the children progress along the path towards a significant number of Early Learning Goals for language and literacy development.

While natural, spontaneous conversation is important, you also need to be aware of the specific elements that make up speaking and listening skills. This awareness is useful

if you are to make the most of natural conversation with the children. It is also important in enabling you to plan a suitable range of activities to help the child's progress. These elements include learning new words, developing conversational skills, learning how to listen to others and speaking in a group.

New words

A baby starts absorbing language from birth onwards. By the time she enters nursery or pre-school, she is at her most receptive when it comes to learning new words. While there are a number of vocabulary increasing activities that you can plan for the children in your group (see page 30), you should also look out for one-off opportunities to introduce a new word as part of your natural and spontaneous conversations. For example, on a wet, rainy play-time, ask the little group gathered around you to *avoid* the puddles and demonstrate by walking carefully around them. When Sophie comes up to show you the raindrop-covered cobweb she has spotted, say how *delicate* it is. The context of the setting and your actions will help the children understand and retain the meaning of the words. You can also have great fun introducing similes, metaphors and interesting adjectives, both as planned language activities (see pages 60 and 62) and within your everyday conversations -

'I'm as cold as an ice lolly'; 'Look at the raindrops on the fence - they're sparkling like diamonds'.

Books, rhymes, finger play and songs are another important means of extending vocabulary. The story and pictures often help the child to make sense of an unfamiliar word and the fact that the book can be read again and again allows for repeated exposure to the new word in its meaningful context. Look out for new words and new meanings of familiar words to highlight and explain to the children. While young children are good at questioning things that do not make sense to them, it is less common for them to ask about an unfamiliar word before the age of five or six. This means that you have to do a bit of advance thinking about the vocabulary in the stories you plan to read or the rhymes you share with the children. For example, 'Jack fell down and broke his *crown* ....' Most children probably hold an interpretation of crown in their minds, ranging from the hat the queen wears to the tissue paper creation that came out of the cracker at Christmas. Here is an opportunity to explain to the children that in this nursery rhyme, crown means head. Put it in context for them by trying out the substitute word: 'Jack fell down and broke his head.'

The Early Learning Goals for speaking and listening recognise the importance of vocabulary enrichment, with the requirement that most children should be able to 'extend their vocabulary, exploring the meanings and sounds of new words' by the end of their reception year. While we all continue gathering new words throughout life, it is during the early years that the foundations are laid. If young children are to develop their vocabularies to the fullest possible extent, you have a significant role to play in helping them learn, explore and enjoy the multitude of words that make up our language.

Becoming a conversationalist

Listening and taking turns in a conversation are essential social and linguistic skills. From the very beginning, parents interact with their babies in ways that help the child develop the ability to converse. The baby gurgles, babbles or produces a syllable. The parent looks into the baby's eyes, smiles and repeats that sound to the baby. Then it is the baby's turn again. Parents do this without thinking, but it is

vital in laying the foundations for appropriate conversational behaviour.

Later, when the child comes to your setting, you can continue helping her to develop as a conversationalist. Always listen carefully to what she says. One of the Early Learning Goals is to 'sustain attentive listening' and you can help the child progress towards this goal by providing a good role model as a listener. There are also many games and activities that help develop the general skill of listening and concentrating on spoken language (see page 46 for some suggestions).

Having listened carefully to the child, make sure you respond in as meaningful a way as possible so that she can then reply to you and continue the conversation. This relates specifically to the Early Learning Goals that require children to respond 'to what they have heard by relevant comments, questions or actions' and 'interact with others ... taking turns in conversation.' In a one-to-one conversation, gently encourage the child to face you and look into your eyes - always best done if you can squat down at the child's eye level. Help the child to answer as fully as possible; one useful technique is to repeat the child's response in natural but fully expanded sentences. For example, Hannah replies to your question about home time: 'Goin' home with James.' You can then respond, 'Yes, Hannah, you're going home with James this afternoon, aren't you?' This provides some early, oral preparation for the writing goal of 'forming simple sentences, sometimes using punctuation.' You can also respond to the child in ways that correct any mistakes, without making her feel corrected. For example, Hannah says: 'I wented to play with James.' You can then reply: 'Yes, Hannah, you went to play with James yesterday, didn't you?' This is a particularly useful technique if you have children in your group for whom English is not their first language, or children whose language development is slow. For these children, as well as for the younger ones, include as much action as possible to help them grasp the meaning of your words. For example, show a child how to put her chair under the table as well as asking her to do so.

Whenever you have the time, extend conversations and discussions for as long as possible. If you have lots of helpful parents and grandparents, draft them in simply to talk and listen to the children - and if they feel they are 'not doing much', reassure them that they couldn't be helping the children more! It is also useful to keep in mind the many different purposes of spoken language and try to create opportunities for the child to describe, express needs, ask questions, answer questions, predict, instruct, explain.... the list could go on and on!

The oral language experiences you provide should include speaking and listening within a group. This helps the children become able to 'speak clearly and audibly with confidence and control and show awareness of the listener'. Useful moments for group discussion include: during or after a story; when someone has a special event to talk about; when an object, event or situation has attracted interest or when an incident takes place that needs discussing with the group. Moments such as these provide rich opportunities to help your

children progress towards the Early Learning Goal of 'using language to imagine and recreate roles and experiences'. In all of these cases, the child's interest is likely to be engaged because the discussion topic is relevant and familiar - which gives her the best possible chance of being able to join in and contribute.

The more knowledge the adult has of the child speaker, the better he or she is able to understand and respond meaningfully to the child. This is common sense, of course - but it's not always easy to achieve in the early years setting. You cannot know the children or their experiences as intimately as their parents, and sometimes it's difficult to respond meaningfully to the child when she wants to discuss something you know nothing about. What you can do is try to learn as much about the child's life as possible, in order to help your conversational responses. This is particularly important if you have children whose home language is not English, or

children with special needs. Sensitively encourage the parents of these children to tell you about their home lives, family outings, trips, events - although take care not to appear too intrusive. The other point to bear in mind is the value of encouraging parents to converse with their children as much as possible. Some parents are reassured to discover that they really are the best people in the world to help their children develop language skills. They need no special training or knowledge, just the time and the will to chat with their children about anything and everything under the sun!

Books

Babies Need Books Dorothy Butler (Penguin) ISBN 0 14 010094 6 Readable; gives lots of advice and recommendations for choosing books, from birth to six.

The Teaching of Reading Jeni Riley (Paul Chapman) ISBN 1 85396 307 0 Gives a clear theoretical explanation and lots of practical advice on the teaching of literacy in the early years.

Understanding Children's Development Peter Smith and Helen Cowie (Blackwell) ISBN 0 631 17792 2 A clear introduction to all aspects of child development.

Young Children Learning Barbara Tizard and Martin Hughes (Fontana) ISBN 0 00 686131 8 An extensive study, comparing child/adult conversation at home with nursery school - all early years workers should be aware of the findings. Readable and enjoyable as well as thought-provoking.

The development of speaking and listening skills – what to expect

When a child first enters nursery or pre-school, her listening and comprehension skills will probably be quite limited. Many children have not yet developed to the point where they can understand and follow verbal instructions. So, for example, you cannot ask the very young child to put her mat on the pile and then assume that she will be able to assimilate and act on this instruction. She needs to be shown, possibly again and again until she has absorbed the routine. Gradually, she will become better able to listen and her ability to respond to verbal instructions will become much more reliable, although never assume that any child has understood and retained information where matters of health, hygiene and safety are concerned.

When it comes to listening to stories, the children who arrive in your setting will probably fall into one of three broad categories: the children who have already had lots of books at home and can listen well, even at a young age; the children who have yet to discover the joy of stories but will do so and learn to listen and concentrate; and the children who, for a variety of reasons, may never become particularly 'bookish'. In the third case, the lack of interest often stems from the desire to be 'up and doing.' These are the children who benefit most from one-to-one story times, short sessions and carefully chosen subject matter that relates to their own interest and experience.

As with all aspects of development, the children vary enormously in how long they can sit and listen to a story. By the time they leave pre-school, many should be able to manage ten or even fifteen minutes - longer in some cases, and certainly longer in an individual or small group situation.

Speaking skills also vary enormously. During the early years, discussing a theme or topic involves quite a lot of effort on your part to help the children keep to the point. By the time older ones are ready to move on to reception class, many will be less likely to go off at a tangent, particularly if they have done lots of group discussion work. If a child's speech development seems a little slow, take into account whether understanding of the spoken word is good, before getting too anxious. If a child is not speaking clearly, try to listen out for common problems such as missing the first sound from a word (so that 'spoon' is pronounced 'poon', for example), or difficulties in pronouncing a particular sound. Identifying a pronunciation difficulty helps you to understand the child's speech and you can also then give her practice in reproducing the problem sound.

Tempting as it is to use ages as a guide for what children should or shouldn't be doing, it is ultimately much more beneficial if you can listen, observe and help each child to develop from the point she is at, rather than pushing her to achieve a pre-ordained stage in her speaking and listening skills.

The area of learning explained

Becoming a reader

Reading

Reading is one of the most important aspects of the Language and Literacy area of learning. It is a hugely complex process, demanding a wide network of knowledge and skills. Because of this complexity, any language and literacy based work has the potential to help the child's development as a reader - even if reading does not appear to be a direct aim of the activity. It is also reassuring to remember that most early reading skills will emerge naturally and spontaneously - as long as you can provide valuable and supportive learning experiences for the children in your care. The following sections look at some of the key areas of importance in helping your children develop into literate individuals.

Oral preparation

Talking and listening do not just help the oral skills of conversation and increase of vocabulary. Preparation for independent reading is also rooted in the language that surrounds the baby and young child, starting at the very beginning with those first shared gurgles. The child uses many strategies once she becomes an independent reader. One of the most important is her natural understanding of language, absorbed through speaking and listening to adults and other children. For example, her knowledge of word meaning will tell her that the word she has just read does not seem to fit into the sentence. Her knowledge of how words go together (syntax) helps her to predict what might come next in the sentence she is reading. Both of these skills alert her to the need to try again

if what she has read does not make sense. These are not techniques the child is aware of. It is simply knowledge that she has absorbed naturally and uses automatically in her attempt to understand what she is reading. We can help the child in this area by immersing her in lots of oral language activities and natural, spontaneous conversation.

Written language

Access to a wide variety of good picture books and other forms of written language is also essential to reading

development. (The term 'picture book' refers to a book containing words and pictures, and in some instances, pictures alone.) Written language is different from spoken language. The child needs to be read to as much as possible, to become familiar with the patterns of stories, poems and so on. When a particular book takes off with your group, try to re-read it as often as possible and then make it available in the book corner. Remind the children

that they can go and look at the book by themselves. Many a young child has sat down and 'read' a book with great enjoyment because they know it so well. It doesn't matter at this stage that they are 'reading' from memory - the important thing is that the child is using books and seeing herself as a reader.

While written language is quite different from spoken language, the language patterns in good picture books reflect those of everyday speech. What child doesn't hear tones of mum or dad in John Burningham's

wonderful *Mr Gumpy's Outing?* ' "Can I come along Mr Gumpy?" said the rabbit. "Yes, but don't hop about." ' The good picture book uses natural language rather then the stilted sentence structures and word repetitions of the reading scheme. Because of this, it is much more likely to grab the child's interest, both as a listener and, later on, as an independent reader. Such books also provide a bridge between oral and written language. The child is not yet able independently to access the words on the page of *Mr Gumpy's Outing*, but hearing it read aloud makes sense to her because the language is natural and familiar.

While books and poems are a hugely important part of the young child's learning, written language crops up all over the place - shop names, print on packages, magazines, newspapers, notices, labels on doors, birthday cards ..... The child has been surrounded by print from babyhood. Capitalise on this by introducing the children to as many different forms of written language as possible. Label anything that 'needs' a label. This doesn't include 'table' or 'book' unless you are doing a specific reading/writing activity, but you could label unfamiliar objects on the nature table, or the box of spare crayons, or the place where finished work is stored. Add little descriptions, such as an explanation of the hyacinth bulb on the window sill. Read these to the children to expand their experience of written language. Better still, discuss with the children what to say and write down their suggestions. Read the print on the biscuit packet and juice carton before snack time. Read the recipe with the children before a cooking activity. Read the instructions on the box of a new game.

If you take your children swimming or on a visit, draw their attention to notices, names, lists of rules, signposts - any form of written language. Apart from helping them to realise the purpose of written language, you will be giving them an experience of the different styles of written language. A Robert Louis Stevenson poem is quite different from the recipe for baking muffins - but both are written language with a message to convey

The purpose of books

Part of becoming a successful reader involves finding out about the purpose of books. It is only through practical experience that the child can make these discoveries. Stories can be fun and pleasurable. They can be relaxing, exciting, frightening, thought provoking. Books can tell you more about what you already know or introduce new information. They can be used with a friend, with a grown-up, by yourself, in a group. They come in all shapes and sizes and can be found at school, at home, in the bookshop, in the library.

To help the child discover what books are all about, introduce as wide a variety as possible - stories, poems, word books, dictionaries, factual books, wordless books. Factual books are important in showing children the potential of books to inform us and answer our questions. This links with the Early Learning Goal that says children should, by the end of the reception year, be able to demonstrate 'understanding of how information can be found in non-fiction texts, to answer questions about where, who, why and how'. Remember also the role of information technology. For the young child of today, literacy includes being able to access the written word and image on the computer for similar purposes of pleasure and information.

Awareness of narrative

Awareness of how books work as physical objects and a sense of story are also important elements in helping your children become whole readers. Show the children how to find their way around books, starting with fundamental skills such as lifting the book from the shelf and putting it back, carrying the book safely and turning pages. Observe your new children with books and see what little practical skills they need help with. As the children become ready, name the different parts of the book. Ultimately, you can look at concepts such as author or publisher. One of the best ways of discovering about writing, illustrating and making a book is for the children to do it themselves and some ideas for this activity are given later. (See 'I'm an author!', page 54).

Narrative awareness is another important reading skill. This sounds rather a grand term for little ones, but all it means is developing a sense of how stories work. Gradually, and through exposure to books, the child becomes familiar with story elements such as the beginning, the ending and typical story events such as a 'threat', a 'change' or a 'cause and effect' situation. This links with the Early Learning Goal for the children to 'show an understanding of elements of stories, such as main character, sequence of events, and openings...' We can sometimes overlook the importance of this goal in helping the child become a wholly literate reader. Just as having an understanding of language helps the child predict and judge what comes next in the line of print she is reading, so a sense of how a story works helps her to judge what might come on the next page or at the end of the story. The understanding and enjoyment that narrative awareness brings is essential to reading because it is what inspires the child to carry on to the end - and then go on to read other books.

The occasional child may reach this stage of reading whole books during his or her pre-school years. For the majority, however, you need to think in terms of preparation and laying foundations for later reading. Like most pre-school learning, narrative awareness is something that happens spontaneously if you can offer the children an appropriate range of experiences. (See page 26 for specific activities that help children develop their understanding of story.)

Awareness of sound

One of the fundamental skills the child needs to develop in order to become a reader is phonemic awareness. This relates to the Early Learning Goal of being able to 'hear and say initial and final sounds in words, and short vowel sounds within words'. Phonemic awareness means the ability to recognise the different sounds that make up our language. A phoneme is the smallest unit of sound in a language. The sounds represented by the letters of the alphabet are all phonemes, as are those sounds represented by digraphs (two letters that make a new sound when put together, such as sh, th, ai, oa). The word *coat* has three phonemes: c-oa-t. The word *bottle* has four: b-o-t-l.

The rhythms of nursery rhymes, jingles, songs and books with rhyming texts play an essential role in helping your children develop awareness of sound. There is a strong link between the ability to detect and produce rhymes and alliteration (where several words begin with the same sound - for example, 'Georgy, **P**orgy, **p**udding and **p**ie') and early success in reading. Fortunately, most young children cannot get enough of rhymes and jingles! Recite and sing from memory, read them from books, play tapes of nursery rhymes, clap them, skip them, add finger plays and movements, use them in large groups, small groups and one to one on the spur of the moment.

Look out for special opportunities. A spider in the sink? A good excuse for 'Incy Wincy Spider'. Puddles in the playground? Time for 'Dr Foster went to Gloucester'. Later in this book, suggestions are given for sound games and jingles that encourage the children to create their own rhythms and rhymes, and for poetry making where they can play with alliteration (see pages 40 - 'I Spy with a difference', and 60 - 'Water poems'). The word play is important here. Fun and enjoyment are the key words for learning at this stage in the child's life and they particularly love turning their

established view of the world upside down with nonsense verse as well as playfully exploring the sounds, rhythms and rhymes of language.

Alphabet books are also valuable in helping children focus on the initial sounds in words. To help them move towards the Early Learning Goal of 'linking sounds to letters' look out for alphabets that show clearly the letter symbol. Ideally, the letter should be printed in both upper and lower case (Mm, Pp).

If you are relying on an alphabet book as a first introduction to the sounds of the 26 letters, choose something clear and simple with just one object for each letter/sound and check that the object tallies with the sound (**a**pple rather than **a**pricot for a, **i**nk rather than **i**ce cream for i.) Publishers come up with all sorts of ways to deal with the tricky letter **x**. The most authentic from the point of view of letter sounds is to move from the initial letter format and go for 'bo**x**' or 'fo**x**'.

As soon as possible, introduce range and variety. There are many wonderful alphabets to choose from. Share as many as you can with the children and, as with all books, put them in your book corner so the children can look at them independently. Ideas are given later in this book for making your own alphabets with the children in your group (see page 52). Collectively, this work will help your children towards the Early Learning Goal of 'naming and sounding the letters of the alphabet.'

I can read!

Along with learning to recognise the sounds that make up words, the child needs to start matching the letters of the alphabet with the sounds they represent. This relates to the Early Learning Goal of 'linking sounds to letters'. As she gains more experience of written language, she will also

increase her sight vocabulary of common digraphs such as th, sh or oa, common letter clusters such as spr, rch or air and common words. The more you encourage the child to look at and share books, the more she is exposed to the building blocks that make up language. This, combined with specific activities, helps the child progress towards the goal of independent reading (see 'I can read' activities on pages 50-51 for some suggestions).

There are various ways in which the child approaches the printed word when she actually starts to read independently. Reading a simple, phonetic word such as *cat* involves recognising the sound made by each letter, and blending the sounds together to read that word as a whole. So, the sounds *c*, *a* and *t* become the word *cat*. This is known as a phonic approach to reading. It can be a good starting point for some children in giving them an initial positive reading experience. It is also a useful word attack strategy for later in the child's reading career. Phonics has not always been well regarded by the experts, but if you ask an eleven-year-old with poor phonic knowledge to tackle an unfamiliar word, you soon discover that she can't even get started!

The main problem with phonics is that it doesn't help much with the thousands of English words that are not phonetic - *the, we* and *why* to give just three common examples. In order to deal with words such as these, the child needs to build up a sight vocabulary and the ability to use context in helping her decipher a word. It is also worth bearing in mind that some children never cope particularly well with the logical and analytical skills of phonics and respond better to absorbing the whole word. Once again, the best approach here is to give the child as much exposure to written language as possible. Interestingly, research shows that picture books make far greater use of the most common English words than reading schemes. At this early stage, don't worry about structured reading schemes if the child is getting plenty of access to good picture books. Make the most of your partnership with parents and send books and book lists home at the end of each session, as well as encouraging parents to visit the library with their children.

Eventually, the reader becomes able to read everything by sight - even phonetic words that the child might initially have read by recognising the symbols and blending their sounds. Again, this fluency comes from practice. The more you read, the quicker and more skilful you become. While you should be flexible in your expectations of the pre-school child, it is important to remember that the foundations are laid during the early years, regardless of what level the child has reached when she begins compulsory schooling.

The whole picture

Many skills come together to create the whole reader. In order to interpret the written symbols on the page, the child uses the mechanics of phonic awareness and recognition of common words, letter clusters and digraphs. She uses her knowledge of word meaning and syntax to help her predict what might come next and judge whether she has read correctly. She uses narrative awareness, context, pictures and her own understanding of the world to construct meaning and make sense of what she reads. She uses her experience of a wide variety of books and written language to assess the purpose and intention of what she has read. And all of these skills and capabilities add to the enjoyment and pleasure she gains because they give her mastery over the printed word.

The development of reading skills – what to expect

Some children will sit and look at books from the moment they arrive at pre-school or nursery. Ideally, you should aim for every child to have realised the pleasure to be gained from books by the time he or she leaves your setting. This will be demonstrated through the child's interest in listening to stories and willingness to sit down and get in amongst the pages of a book.

In relation to the actual skill of reading, the child can begin phonemic or sound awareness games and activities as soon as she enters the early years setting (see 'I spy with a difference', page 38). Children vary considerably when it comes to hearing the sounds that make up words. Once the child can recognise the initial sounds, the ability to hear end sounds often follows on quickly and causes great excitement. If you choose to do lots of sound and letter matching activities with those children who are ready, you may find that some can start reading simple phonetic words before they leave the pre-school setting and certainly during their reception year. These children will probably also be absorbing some of the common non-phonetic words such as 'the' or 'here', simply through exposure to written language. At this point, you can try introducing games to help the child learn more of these words (see 'I can read!' - page 50). This relates to the Early Learning Goal requiring children to 'read a range of familiar and common words and simple sentences independently' by the end of their reception year.

In a few rare cases, children at the pre-school stage will reach something approaching the status of a 'whole reader'. The vast majority will reach various points along the path towards whole reading during their time with you. It is essential to recognise that the pre-school/reception-age child is still very young. If a child is not ready for reading related activities, she should not be pushed, whatever outside pressures you might feel subject to. For those who are ready, it is fine for them to progress along the path towards whole reading at this early stage. For those who are not, the long-term effects of too much pressure could well be disastrous when it comes to developing confidence and a love of reading.

Becoming a writer

Writing

The skills of reading and writing are closely linked. Basic, mechanical knowledge of sounds and their matching letters is needed for both reading and writing. Thus, much of the work you do in preparing children to read will, at the same time, be helping to prepare them for writing. In many ways, writing is easier than reading and it is not uncommon for writing to emerge before reading - if the child is in a setting that encourages and enables this form of expression. Whereas reading involves interpreting someone else's thoughts, writing involves setting down your own thoughts so that you are starting out from a position of knowledge.

Like reading, writing is a complex process made up of many different strands. There are three general areas of capability the child needs to develop:

❑ The ability to decide the content of what you want to say in terms of the message, the words you use and how you organise the words so that they make sense (syntax).

❑ The ability to analyse the sounds that make up the words and represent them with appropriate letters.

❑ The ability to hold and control the writing implement in order to reproduce those letters on paper.

What shall I write?

When it comes to the content of the writing, the child's experience of oral language and written language in all its forms comes into play. A good vocabulary and knowing how words fit together to create meaningful sentences will help the child with what she wants to say. If she has had experience of a wide variety of written language, she will know that she can write lists, notes, messages, letters, poems, instructions, recipes, signs, stories..... the possibilities are endless.

In the case of stories, the narrative awareness that is so important to the development of reading is also essential to the child as a writer. Children are capable of telling stories from a very young age and often these stories are informed by the books they have shared with adults. You can build on this by making a wide range of book-related resources, props and techniques available to the children to help them to role play and retell the stories they have listened to (see page 27 - 'Story time' and page 66 - 'Role play activities'). This contributes towards the Early Learning Goals of 'using language to imagine and recreate roles and experiences' and 'retell narratives in the correct sequence, drawing on the language patterns of stories.' Join in as one of the characters in the story if you feel that the children need a little guidance - although this is best avoided if you have new children in the group as they are still establishing your identity as a recognisable and safe adult in this strange environment.

Of course, the child is able to come up with thoughts, ideas and stories long before she is capable of setting the words down on paper. You can enable her to engage in this aspect of the writing process simply by writing down these thoughts on her behalf. This can range from a simple statement about a painting to an extended story, written within a group or individually (see page 36 - 'Dictation'). Another alternative is to introduce a tape recorder to the children so that they can record their stories orally. The recordings can then be played back and transcribed, to give the children the opportunity to revisit their thoughts in two different forms - oral and written. These activities help the children towards the Early Learning Goal of 'attempt(ing) writing for various purposes, using features of different forms such as lists, stories, instructions.'

From thoughts to symbols

In order to get the words onto the paper in written form, the child has to be able to analyse the sounds that make up a word and represent those sounds with letters and combinations of letters. So, if she wants to write the word *cat*, she has to be able to separate the word into its constituent sounds c-a-t and then match each sound with its appropriate letter. At this stage in the child's development as a writer, it is important that she is allowed to write for herself as much as possible. This tallies with the Early Learning Goal of 'using phonic knowledge to write simple regular words and make phonetically plausible attempts at more complex words.' 'Phonetically plausible' means writing a word in a way that makes sense, given the child's phonic knowledge. If a child wrote the word 'because' as 'bcoz', this would show that she has a good knowledge of sounds and symbols - a different thing altogether from knowledge of spelling. At this stage, spelling does not matter. This will come later as the child absorbs the correct spelling for words through reading. The odd spellings the child produces as she bases her writing on her current phonic knowledge will not fix themselves permanently in her mind as they are flowing out rather than in.

During the early years, the child may be ready to symbolise words before she can easily form the letters with a writing implement. You can get over this obstacle by giving her a set of cut-out or plastic letters to 'write' with. This means that she is only having to address one aspect of the complex writing process. Another option, if you have a computer or word processor, is to show the child how to type letters to create words. As with a cut-out alphabet, all the child has to do is recognise the appropriate letter so that it removes the challenge of using the writing implement. It also helps the development of IT skills by familiarising the child with the keyboard. Unless you have done a lot of work with capitals, put stickers with the lower case letters on the keys.

Putting pencil to paper

Having decided what she wants to say and how to translate her thoughts into written symbols, the child then has to form the appropriate letters on the page with a writing implement. This means being able to hold and control the pencil in order to write the letters. Any activity that develops hand/eye co-ordination and muscular control is helpful here - playing with Duplo or Lego, building towers with bricks, pouring water from a jug, tipping sand from a spade into a bucket. Other activities have a more direct relationship with writing. Puzzles with knobs on use the index and thumb,

the two main digits that grip and guide the writing implement. Finger painting, traditional painting, drawing, colouring, chalking on the blackboard are all activities that train the hand to control a mark maker. Children can be encouraged to explore writing patterns, particularly with finger painting. Buy thick finger paint or mix it with wallpaper paste (checking first that it is non-toxic). Show the children how to create patterns based on the way that letters are formed - circles, semi-circles, zig-zags, vertical, horizontal and slanted lines, arches, waves, loops. This is important preparation for the Early Learning Goal of being able to 'use a pencil and hold it effectively to form recognisable letters.' (Some suggestions for how to introduce writing letters are given on page 48.)

The whole picture

Ultimately, we are working towards a child who knows what to say, how to express herself, how to translate those thoughts into symbolic form and how to represent those symbols on the paper. The preparation and process is inextricably linked with reading. When we talk about somebody being literate, we mean that they have mastery over both reading and writing.

Apart from planned activities, spontaneous conversations and story-times, you can create an environment that encourages and provides opportunities for writing as a part of play. See pages 22-25 for some ideas on how to introduce writing materials into the home corner and the book corner, and also for creating a writing corner.

The development of writing – what to expect

As with many of the language and literacy skills, the ability to grip a pencil well enough to form letters varies from child to child. Some arrive at nursery with a perfect grip, others

struggle. Between three and four years, most children start learning to write their own names so that the name is recognisable at least in parts. One of the Early Learning Goals for Writing requires the children to be able to 'write their own names' by the end of the reception year.

Once you and your children have played lots of sound awareness games, you can introduce the activity of matching sounds and letters. If the child responds well to this, you can continue steadily, with the possibility that the child will be able to recognise many or even all of the letter sounds and some digraphs by the time she leaves your setting. If the child does not respond well, leave the activity for the time being.

Older children may start attempting to write simple, phonetic words and common non-phonetic words from memory (such as *the* or *you*). They may also begin to make reasonable attempts at less common non-phonetic words. However, this will depend on the preparation work you have done with your group and what they are ready for. This degree of writing ability should not be regarded as an aim for all children by the time they leave a pre-school setting or nursery, although it does constitute one of the Early Learning Goals for the end of the reception year: 'most children will be able to use their phonic knowledge to write simple, regular words and make phonetically plausible attempts at more complex words'.

As with all aspects of the young child's learning and development, the key to giving the best possible support for speaking and listening, reading and writing is to recognise and follow the needs of each individual child.

Links with other areas of learning

The child is constantly developing her language and literacy skills. She thinks through language; she communicates through language; she learns through language - and as we have seen, any language development also helps her growing literacy skills. As a result of this, language and literacy intermesh with all other areas of learning: Personal, Social and Emotional Development, Mathematical Development, Creative Development, Knowledge and Understanding of the World, even Physical Development.

Personal, Social and Emotional Development

The goals for this learning area cover the child's personal, social, emotional, moral and spiritual development. Language and literacy are of paramount importance in enabling the child's learning and development on both the inner personal and the outer social levels. Along with creative work (art, drama, music, dance), Language and Literacy is the area of learning that most readily lends itself to exploring the many personal, social and emotional issues that crop up daily in the early years setting.

Establishing good attitudes to learning

The Early Learning Goals for Personal, Social and Emotional Development include the establishment of good attitudes to learning, with goals such as the child becoming 'interested, excited and motivated to learn'. They also overlap with some of the Language and Literacy goals. For example,

developing the ability to 'maintain attention, concentrate and sit quietly when appropriate' is similar to the goal of 'sustain(ing) attentive listening.'

The best way of helping young children to reach these goals is to engage their interest - and language is one of the most powerful means at our disposal. Talk to your children in ways they can understand, while at the same time offering new thoughts and ideas. Use all methods of communication to

attract their attention. The majority of little ones are easily won over if your facial expressions, body language and the tone of your voice suggest that something is exciting, interesting and worth listening to. Plan language and literacy activities so that they suit the level and interests of the children in your group. Story time is particularly useful; as long as you have chosen your book carefully and possess reasonable story reading skills, you have an immediate head start because the book

is a resource designed to capture and hold the attention of young children.

The role of language in social and emotional development

It is largely through language that the specifically social goals of this area of learning can be achieved. Whenever you discuss behaviour, such as being kind to one another, you are using language to help the children with the Early Learning Goal of 'developing awareness of their own needs, views and feelings and being sensitive to the needs, views and feelings of others'. Likewise, it is through small group discussions that you and your children can successfully consider and negotiate the 'agreed values and codes of behaviour' that are necessary for your group 'to work together harmoniously'. Children always learn best in a context that is interesting and meaningful to them. Behaviour related topics are particularly relevant to the child because they are to do with her own experiences, environment and social group.

The ability to 'form good relationships with peers and adults' is central to the child's social development and, hence, one of the most significant of the Early Learning Goals.

The Scottish Curriculum Framework also suggests that a child should 'begin to develop particular friendships with other children'. Conversation is vital in enabling the children to connect everyone in their family, school and wider social group. It also helps them learn to 'consider the consequences of their words and actions, for themselves and others'. As other people make conversational responses, so the child discovers that words have great power to comfort or wound, create a sense of belonging or alienate, cause joy and pleasure or sadness.

Learning the conventions of social language can greatly increase the child's skills and confidence in this area. If you know how and when to say 'please', 'thank you' and so on, it helps to smooth your passage through certain social events and situations. Try out some little role play activities with your children, to help them learn how to behave thoughtfully and with confidence in their dealings with other people. For example, place a table close to a wall so that there is only a small space in between and position an adult in the space so that the child has to say 'Excuse me, please' in order to get past. Later, the children can take on both roles. Observe your children to help you decide which little social graces need practice - the 'Excuse me, please' activity is particularly useful if you have a lot of little 'bargers' in your group!

These little role play activities can hold a special value for children who do not have English as their first language. Learning social language and routines is an important means of fitting into an unfamiliar group or culture. You can also invite members from a variety of communities into your setting, to help introduce your children to social conventions from other cultures. This has the two-fold benefit of providing a link between home and school for the children from these communities, and introducing the rest of your group to different cultural traditions and practices. It also helps the children towards the Early Learning Goals of 'developing respect for their own cultures and beliefs and those of other people' and developing the understanding that 'people have

different needs, views, cultures and beliefs, which need to be treated with respect.'

Meal times and table behaviour are an important part of every culture. The Northern Ireland Curricular Guidance for Pre-school Education suggests that adults make the most of such occasions to talk 'naturally and informally with the children about healthy foods and healthy eating habits'. This is an important element of the child's personal development. Snack times and lunch times can also be valuable as sociable occasions, providing some good opportunities for general conversation and gentle reinforcement of appropriate meal-time behaviour.

Any discussion-based activity will support the child's progress towards the goal of 'taking turns and sharing fairly' - in this case, the sharing of time and attention. Group activities such as news time (see page 34) are also useful in helping the child become 'confident to try things, initiate ideas and speak in a group'. Drama groups, role play and story-telling can all contribute to the child's developing ability to 'work as part of a group or class' - a goal that relates both to social development and attitudes to learning.

Using picture books

Picture books play an important role in helping the child's personal, social and emotional development. Many stories revolve around a moral issue, exploring the choices available to us in everyday life through the story and its characters. This makes them a useful resource in working towards the Early Learning Goal of 'understand(ing) what is right, what is wrong, and why'. Compile a list of the books that deal with moral issues in a way that is interesting and relevant to the young child. You can then help the children to make the most of the story with discussions and role play. Ask the children: 'What would you have done?'

and use their responses as a basis for discussion. This helps them to progress towards the goal of having a 'developing awareness of their own needs, views and feelings and being sensitive to the needs, views and feelings of others'.

A good book can be useful in helping a child with a specific life challenge or significant experience. There is a picture book available to cover just about everything, from the upheaval of moving house to the death of a family member. The best ones incorporate the theme into a story although there are some carefully planned and attractive information books aimed at young children. Books can also help your children aspire to the Early Learning Goal of 'developing respect for their own cultures and beliefs and those of other people' and developing the understanding that 'people have different needs, views, cultures and beliefs, which need to be treated with respect'. It is important that the books in your book corner reflect the racial and cultural mix of your group, but remember also the value of these books in helping children learn about unfamiliar cultures. The four-year-old white boy growing up in rural England needs stories about the four-year-old black girl growing up in the inner city - and vice versa. Ideally, you should invite adults from different communities and races into your setting to talk to your children about their cultures, beliefs, legends, food. Failing that, a good book is the next best thing.

As you choose books to read to your group throughout the year, try to consider the possible emotional reactions that each book might inspire in the children. This relates to the Early Learning Goal of responding 'to significant experiences, showing a range of feelings when appropriate'. It is not always appropriate to organise or easy to pick up on real life events that elicit feelings, such as joy, wonder or sympathy. The good picture book is useful here in that it has the potential to inspire all these feelings, and you can plan ways of making the most of the emotional experience through discussion, art work, music and dance, role play, retelling or acting out the story with devices such as flannel boards and cut-outs or props and dressing-up clothes (see page 22). Aim to cover the full emotional range in the books you share with the children. For example, humour is appealing, but young children also need opportunities to respond to other types of literature, such as beautiful, thought-provoking pictures and poetic language.

As you trawl through the library or the bookshop, you may come across books that make you feel uncomfortable. If you are not happy about the way in which a book handles a sensitive topic, then avoid it, whatever the blurb on the back cover says. The children will pick up on your unease at a time when you most need to be confident and reassuring. Where sensitive matters are concerned, it is much better to share the book with an individual or small group. This will enable you to pick up on and deal with any distress that you might miss in a larger group.

Personal, Social and Emotional Development is a pre-requisite for success in all other learning areas, as well as essential if the child is to function properly within the family, school group and society as a whole. When you are feeling particularly hard pressed, take comfort in the fact that virtually all of your language and book based work will help one or other of the Personal, Social and Emotional Development Goals.

Mathematical Development

Mathematics is an area of learning that does not always intermesh with Language and Literacy in obvious ways. Nevertheless, if we dig beneath the surface, we find a number of important and interesting similarities.

Number is a symbol system - and so is language. Take the phrase 'three cakes.'

Numerically, we represent the quantity of cakes with the word 'three' (a symbol), and we represent the word 'three' with the number '3' (a further symbol). Linguistically, we represent the object with the spoken word 'cake' (a symbol) and we represent that word in writing - c-a-k-e (a further symbol). Both maths and language therefore demand the ability to understand and use representative symbol systems.

The human mind is well equipped to learn, understand and use such systems. The young child begins exploring a wide range of symbols from a very early age. Play is perhaps the most important means of developing this important ability, with toys and picture books as one of the child's earliest experiences of representative objects. For example, when the child plays with her toy

cooker, she is not using the real thing but a representation, albeit a very obvious one. The importance of other play activities in relation to symbolic representation are explored later (see page 25).

Mathematics does not just involve number. Concepts such as volume, distance, length and capacity are all mathematical - and all described through language. So, the child makes a mathematical judgement that the jug is 'full' or that the cake is 'larger than' the bun - and she uses language to formulate and describe these judgements. The Early Learning Goal that relates to this branch of mathematics requires the child to 'use language such as "more" or "less", "greater" or "smaller", "heavier" or "lighter" to compare two numbers or quantities'. Another language-related goal is for the child to use 'everyday words to describe position'. This means prepositions such as 'under', 'above', 'behind' and so on (see page 33). Naming and describing shapes and their properties is also word based and relates to the requirement to 'use language such as "circle" or "bigger" to describe the shape and size of solids and flat shapes'. Similarly, the child's early, practical experiences of addition and subtraction will occur through language - 'If Jane gives me 1 sweet, and Ann gives me 2 sweets, how many sweets have I got altogether?' This is what is meant by the Early Learning Goal: 'in practical activities and discussion the children begin to use the vocabulary involved in adding and subtracting'.

Books have an important role to play in helping the young child develop knowledge and understanding of mathematical concepts. There are many excellent books focussing on concepts such as number, shape difference and size. It is also worth keeping in mind the more subtle (but equally useful) ways in which stories embody mathematical concepts. For example, John Burningham's *Mr Gumpy's Outing* or Eric Carle's *The Very Hungry Caterpillar* are, like many stories, based on a clear sequence of events, as well as having the potential for counting activities. David McKee's *Elmer the Elephant* books revolve around the concept of difference. Pat Hutchins' *Titch* explores size. If you share these stories with the children, you will be helping their mathematical development, as well as language and literacy, and elements of their personal, social and emotional growth.

Creative Development

This covers a range of skills and activities, including drama, dance, art and design and music. This area of learning also incorporates the use and development of the imagination and creative expression.

Apart from art work, language is the most obvious means by which young children express their imaginative ideas. The importance of language is recognised through the Early Learning Goal for Creative Development which requires the children to 'express and communicate their ideas, thoughts and feelings ...' Another goal for this area is to 'respond in a variety of ways to what they see, hear, smell, touch and feel'. Any help we can give to the children in expanding their vocabularies and oral expression will also furnish them with the tools needed to make these creative responses and communicate their thoughts and imaginings.

Activities such as role play, drama, singing, story-telling and poetry writing all need language in order to bring them to life. Look out also for the creative possibilities that can emerge from books, to help the children

towards the Early Learning Goal of 'us(ing) their imagination in art and design, music, dance, imaginative and role play, stories and play.' Paintings, drawings, model and puppet making can all be inspired by a good picture book, as can dance, singing, music, imaginative and role play and drama. You can then come full circle by using the results of creative work (puppets, models and so on) to explore and retell the story. Similarly, the child can further explore literacy and language through the creative activities of dance, drama and music. (See page 66.)

Knowledge and Understanding of the World

As with all areas of learning, the child accesses information about the world largely through language. The Early Learning Goals for Knowledge and Understanding of the World include requirements such as the ability to 'find out about ... living things, objects and events' and 'ask questions about why things happen and how things work.' The child uses oral language to ask these questions and relies on her listening and comprehension skills to absorb and process the answers. As her language skills develop, so does her ability to discover and increase her understanding of the world.

Books are an important means of finding out about all aspects of the world around us. Any contribution to the child's literacy development will also help her ability to access factual and cultural information from books - whether she wants to find out about animals in the zoo, how people live in Africa or what a tractor looks like.

Making discoveries about the world can, in its turn, contribute to the child's language and literacy development. The child learns best when she is interested. Through asking questions and finding out about a topic of special interest, the child is more likely to retain new words and language structures. Similarly, if you

can provide books on topics that particularly attract the child, it gives her a purpose to exploring that book. Some children take to books easily, others don't. In the case of the latter, try searching for topics that hold a special attraction so that the child is drawn into the pages of the book almost without realising.

This is also the area of learning that covers the Early Learning Goals for information technology and computers, with the requirement that children should 'find out about and identify the uses of everyday technology ... and use information and communication technology and programmable toys to support their learning'. Computer software relies on pictures, the written word and, in some cases, the spoken word, all of which relate to language and literacy development. This is a good illustration of how inter-supportive an early years activity can be. A carefully chosen programmable toy or piece of software has the capacity to support language and literacy learning, the ability to use computers and information technology, knowledge and understanding of the world and some elements of personal, social and emotional development.

Physical Development

The aspect of physical development that has particular implications for language and literacy is, of course, the ability to hold and control a pencil. The growth of hand control will feed into the writing goal that requires most children to 'use a pencil and hold it effectively to form recognisable letters...' by the end of their reception year. Thus, any activities that help the child learn to handle tools with increasing control will also help her develop the ability to use a writing implement. Access to crayons, pencils, paint brushes and lots of opportunity to draw and make marks will, in turn, help the general development of fine motor skills.

The importance of play

Much of the child's language and literacy learning takes place through play. Play is a complex behaviour and experts do not always agree as to its definition. It is, however, generally accepted that play is essential to the child's learning and development and that young children will play, whether we adults can agree on what it is they are doing or not!

While we can plan set activities for the children, we do not have quite the same direct influence on play. Perhaps our most important role is to create a setting that inspires, encourages and enables lots of rich play opportunities. This involves two main practical considerations: creating appropriate physical areas in your setting and providing suitable toys and resources.

Play settings

For literacy development, it is important to have a book corner and a writing area. For general language development, the home corner is useful, as are the various play environments that can be created to reflect a recent trip, the topic you are looking at, or the particular interests of your group.

The book corner

Choose the quietest part of the room for your book corner and make sure that it is cosy and welcoming, with a carpet, cushions, pictures and plants. One or two comfortable chairs are also appealing, if you have

the space. Make sure that the books are easily accessible and have a table for displays, such as a collection of books by the same author or on a particular theme or genre. For example, if you and your group are looking at 'People Who Help Us', your display could relate to this theme. Alternatively, you could choose a literary genre, such as a collection of poetry books, humourous books, or textless books.

Let the children make the book corner their own. Encourage them to bring in books from home (although you do need to clarify to both children and parents that books brought in for the book corner are to be shared). Have a

noticeboard on the wall for book related paintings, drawings and posters that the children have produced themselves. Also create a space for story props to encourage the children to act out and retell the stories they have read. Stick a large piece of felt to a board and provide drawn and cut-out figures from a story with a strip of Velcro attached. Encourage older children to make their own figures. You can also add life-sized props so that the children can take on the roles for themselves. For example, if *Mr Gumpy's Outing* has gone down well with your group, put out ears and a tail for each animal in the story, a hat for Mr Gumpy and dressing-up clothes for the two children. Encourage the children to think of their own ways to simulate Mr Gumpy's boat.

If you have one, keep a tape recorder near to the book corner with a store of story tapes and blank tapes so that children can listen to stories and also record their own stories, to be re-visited and transcribed. You do, however, need to establish the difference between the story tapes and the blank tapes, and keep an eye on proceedings - for obvious reasons!

You can also make up story packs for children to take home. These can consist of a plastic folder with the book and a tape with the recorded story (home-made is just as good as commercially bought and much cheaper). You can then add whatever props might encourage related play: cut-out figures, soft toys or objects that relate to the story, paper and pencils for 'writing' or drawing, and so on.

All of these props and resources will encourage play to emerge from the books and stories that your children come across. A story is a great starting point for the child to create her own narrative and the provision of props encourages her to play with the original tale, embellishing and expanding as she makes the story her own.

While the adult traditionally does not take part in the child's play, there are advantages in occasionally getting down on your hands and knees with the children. The best way of introducing new characters or possibilities with the story props is to join in yourself. Older children and teenagers are often much better at playing with little ones than the self-conscious adult. Encourage older brothers and sisters to visit your group on their school's in-service day, and draft in teenagers on work experience from local secondary schools and colleges. They are not quite so far removed from the early years of childhood as the adult and often make inspiring playmates.

The writing corner

Just as the book corner encourages free use of books and provides opportunities for play to emerge from the child's book-based experiences, so the writing corner gives the child freedom to play with and explore the act of writing. Set up a group of tables for your writing corner or area and provide a wide range of writing materials - pencils, markers, different types of pen, erasers, rulers, coloured biros, felt tips, anything that will attract the children and encourage them to explore writing. Display the various writing implements so that the children can easily see what is available, and provide pencil pots so that each child can choose a selection to take to one of the writing tables.

The variety of writing papers you can provide is enormous: writing paper in different sizes and colours, including airmail paper (explain to the children what it is and try to find someone abroad to write to); thin strips of plain paper for lists; cards for notes; yellow self-stick notes and sticky white address labels. These are expensive, but any variation to attract the child's interest and encourage exploration is well worth it. Envelopes and decorated gift tags (encourage the children to make their own) are another important addition. These reinforce to the children that letters and cards usually have a recipient and we need to mark our envelope with the name of the person for whom it is intended. You could also introduce stampers and stickers to decorate writing paper and envelopes, and hole punchers, ribbons and paper-clips for holding together a sheaf of papers. Explore quill pens, sealing wax and slates with older children who can begin to think about writing from long ago. Make a folder for each child's writing work, to be stored in the writing corner. Discuss with them the work they wish to keep in their folder; this will help them to see that their writing is special, as well as encouraging them to make their own value judgements about their work.

If you have the space and the resources, provide a flip-board so that the children can experience writing on a large scale. Alternatively, you could pin a large piece of paper to the wall or spread it out on the floor. A blackboard on an easel with coloured chalks also provides a large-scale writing experience, while single, portable blackboards enable the individual child to sit down and chalk in the traditional writing position.

Include a space for writing and print related displays. For example, see how many samples of different print and print styles you and the children can gather. You could include recipes, knitting patterns, printed food packaging, magazines, comics and newspapers, menus, brochures, take-away leaflets from restaurants, bills, receipts, photographs of shop names. This is a good opportunity to enlist the support of families and include samples of print in different languages and scripts from different cultures. If you have access to a word processing package, you could also show the children numerous print styles through exploring the different font sets. Provide a noticeboard so that children can stick up messages to you and each other. Make a post box, to be emptied at the end of each day by a child designated to be postman or woman (a big red bag or satchel adds to the fun of this role). Letters to each other do not have to be written - a drawing addressed to a friend can be posted into the letter box, as long as an older child or adult has added the name of the recipient.

With the wide range of writing related materials available to us, it is easy to build up a large collection. Try to avoid the temptation of putting everything out at once. Young children are confused and overwhelmed by too much choice. To begin with, set out only a small number of materials and allow the children to explore and become familiar with them before adding new things. Build up the range of materials little by little and ring the changes. Save the more expensive materials for special occasions and attract the children's interest by introducing and discussing a new writing paper or implement before adding it to the materials in your writing corner.

The ultimate aim of the writing corner is to encourage and enable the children to explore and play with writing. The young child does not need the full complement of literacy skills in order to see herself as a writer and develop 'writerly' behaviour. The more

chance she is given to enjoy the act of writing, regardless of her level of expertise, the better chance she has of becoming a skilful and literate writer, later in life.

The home corner and the make believe setting

Every early years setting has a home corner. It plays an important role in language development by giving the children an opportunity to act out and explore social language and language related to home-based situations and events. Look out for ways of introducing literacy opportunities to the home corner. Telephones encourage a particular form of play language; put up a noticeboard and a memo board for shopping lists and notes like the ones found in many kitchens; include a little bookshelf with

books and a magazine and newspaper rack; have a writing desk in the corner. You may decide that the home corner would be a suitable setting for your tape recorder and story tapes. A pretend radio and television could encourage the children to act out the roles of the television character or the radio broadcaster; join in the children's play to get them started as TV presenters or actors!

Other make-believe settings can tap into trips or interests. If you have visited the library recently, set up a librarian's desk near your book corner with tickets, a computer, the 'In' and 'Out' sections, and so on. The railway station, the airport, the fire station, the supermarket or toy shop are just a few examples of play settings you could introduce to your environment. Ideally, you should set up a play area following a trip to one of these places. The children will then have real experiences of events, vocabulary and expressions to draw on and explore in their play. Joining in the play yourself will remind the children of the roles and language they came across on their trip. If you do, watch out for an appropriate moment to withdraw, leaving the children to explore and play freely with their new setting.

Toys and general play

The play settings described above relate quite specifically to language and literacy development. Another significant play element in the early years setting is the child's free exploration of toys and other play resources. This type of general play makes a number of important and interesting contributions to language and literacy development.

Play is a representative act. The fact that it is 'not for real' is one of its main characteristics. When the child plays with toy food, she is playing with a symbol of the real thing. When she makes toy food from Plasticene, she is creating a symbol for the real thing. This understanding of and ability to make and use symbols is an important human ability and it is essential that the child enjoys these play experiences as a preparation for the highly sophisticated symbol system that makes up written language. Similarly, when the child is allowed to draw and paint freely, she is developing her ability to represent things with symbols - a very important precursor to writing.

You should aim to provide a wide range of toys and play resources. Some of these can have a clear connection to the real thing, such as toy food, but there should also be a good variety of more creative materials, including Duplo and Lego, Stickle bricks, wooden bricks, Plasticene and playdough, as well as painting and drawing materials. Whenever your children use these materials to make representative objects (lorries, houses, cutlery, cranes) they are tapping into and developing their ability to create and use representative symbols, with the essential preparation this gives for writing and reading. If they engage in this kind of play with other children, they are also using language to communicate thoughts and ideas, to co-operate and negotiate in bringing their ideas to fruition - all essential linguistic skills, as well as helping social development.

Acting out and telling stories is another important part of free and spontaneous play. As well as providing specific story props in your book corner and planning set story-based activities, watch out for the ways in which children use other toys and resources to create and enact their own stories

through play. This is one of the best ways of assessing the effect a story has had on a child.

When you are busy, it can be tempting to dismiss a group of children as 'only playing'. If they are happily occupied within a general regime of supervision, it gives you the chance to get on with other things such as working with a different group of children or an individual. While this is important to the management of your whole group, do try as much as possible to observe the children at play. Work on developing your ability to watch and listen in without the children realising;

this will often tell you far more about a child's capabilities than her performance in a set group activity. Look out for how successfully and fluently the children are using language - their vocabulary, the complexity of their expression, how well they listen and take turns in a conversation. Make a note of how they are using toys and play materials as representative objects in their play, and how they are bringing story into their play. Include these observations in your records for each child - and always keep in mind how important these play activities are for laying foundations in the field of language and literacy learning.

Story time

Sharing picture books with your children is one of the most valuable, versatile and enjoyable activities. As long as you choose appropriate books and have reasonable story reading skills, they will learn naturally and spontaneously from story time. It is also the best way of satisfying the Welsh Desirable Outcome that children should be able to 'listen to a good story' and the Northern Ireland guidance that they should 'enjoy books'.

Story groups

Story time should be relaxed, with the emphasis on enjoyment. A group of children gathered around your feet on the carpet is cosy and friendly, although you could try a more formal arrangement of chairs if you have one or two who do not settle easily.

Make sure that all the children can see the pictures. If possible, hold the book open on your lap and read upside down, or hold it up to one side so the children can look at the pictures throughout the session. Be aware of how much a picture is holding the children's interest and try not to turn the page until they have finished studying it. Pictures are just as important as words at this stage. They often play a significant part in telling the story and helping the child to make sense of the words.

Another option is to invest in some big books. Although quite expensive, they are useful with a large group of children. If you have one or two regular sized copies as well, the children can take it in turns to follow the story in their own version.

Your reading aloud skills make a useful tool in holding the child's interest. Always read through a book before sharing it with the children, partly to check it is suitable and partly to familiarise yourself with the story in advance. If you know what is coming up, you can vary your voice and facial expressions accordingly. Use your voice to express the mood of the story - soft and quiet for a gentle episode; deep and strong for a scary part. The speed at which you read can also be expressive. There are times when reading slowly fits the meaning, and times when a fast pace builds up the excitement. The pregnant pause at a moment of suspense is another useful technique for holding interest or recovering attention if you have one or two who have strayed!

Explore using different voices for different characters and practise your farmyard impressions and sound effects. These are great fun and help the child to make sense of the story - although try not to become too convincing a tiger, giant or whatever the story demands of you. For the new or nervous children, it can be frightening if you suddenly turn into something completely different!

Reading to individuals

Sharing a book with one or two children holds quite different possibilities from the story group. Although we tend to think of stories as group activities in the early years setting, it is well worth reading with single children as much as possible. On a one-to-one basis, it is easier to pick up on questions and comments, and to help the child make sense of the story. You can then build on those elements in the story that particularly interest her, or which cause confusion. It is also much easier to link with a child in a one-to-one situation. This can be useful for the child with special needs, the child who does not have English as a first language or a child who is not taking to books and story time. The presence of the pictures is important for all of these children as a more immediate form of communication and a shared focus of attention. If a child communicates something and you can see the picture she is talking about, it helps you to understand what she is saying. Similarly, if you base your talk around the picture, the child has a much better chance of understanding you because she can literally see what you are talking about.

Take the opportunity to point to the print from time to time with a finger. If you use the 'reading upside' down technique in story groups, it is quite important to reinforce the normal reading position from time to time. Individual sessions also provide better opportunities for the child to familiarise herself with how a book works and the conventions of print. This links with the Northern Ireland guidance that children should be 'aware that the printed word has meaning and that it should be read from left to right' or the Scottish advice that children should 'understand some of the language and layout of books'.

What age?

When the child first arrives in your setting, you should concentrate solely on helping her develop the ability to listen to and enjoy a story. As her appreciation of books grows, you can start to introduce some book-related activities, to help her develop a sense of story and how it works. These activities contribute directly to the Early Learning Goal of 'show(ing) an understanding of the elements of stories, such as main character, sequence of events, and openings ...'

Literary terms such as 'main character' can sound rather a tall order for little ones. You should not, however, be aiming for young children to recognise and define these narrative techniques - this comes much later in the child's schooling. All you should be doing at this stage is highlighting certain story elements through interesting activities so that the child gradually absorbs a sense of narrative. In practical terms, aim for children who can tell which is the figure in the story whose fortunes we are meant to be following, or who can look forward to and enjoy the ending because they have had lots of previous experience of stories.

Narrative awareness

Sequence of events:

Most stories revolve around a narrative sequence, although some more noticeably than others. Eric Carle's *The Very Hungry Caterpillar* and John Burningham's *Mr Gumpy's Outing* are both based on a sequence of events. The masterful construction of each

story makes it easy for the child to absorb and work with this particular story technique. Try acting out *Mr Gumpy's Outing* to reinforce the order of events that lead to the boat tipping over. Each animal can ask its question and get into the boat, one after the other, and then kick, flap, trample, one after the other, until the boat capsizes and they all fall into the water with a splash! Great fun, and a useful means of involving children in a narrative sequence.

Providing cut-out figures, pictures or story props is another useful means of enabling the child to work with and actively involve herself with a story sequence. Young children love playing

---

What you need:

Narrative awareness - sequence of events

Story props relating to the book you are reading.

Cut-out figures/flannel board related to the book.

Drawing materials and paper for children to make their own props.

---

with pictures of the Very Hungry Caterpillar's food, grouping them and putting them into order. You can also encourage older ones to draw pictures of their own food to play with and set out in sequence - a menu for the Very Hungry Caterpillar to munch his way through during the following week perhaps?

The main character:

Part of making sense of a story includes being able to recognise which character the story is all about. The structure of a well-written story makes this accessible for the young child, and the pictures are essential in giving the child a clearly recognisable figure to focus on, page after page.

You can help the children in this task by talking about the main character in general terms: What does he look like? What clothes is he wearing? What colour is his hair? What is his name? It can be useful to start off with a book where there is only one character, such as *The Very Hungry Caterpillar*. You can then shape the discussion accordingly. The question of what the caterpillar is wearing doesn't apply here, but you could still discuss what he looks like, what he does in the story and his name. Be flexible over where the discussion leads you! If the children recognise that he only has a generic name, perhaps they can come up with their own suggestions: 'I think the Very Hungry Caterpillar's name is Josh ...'

Role play activities are another useful means of focussing on the central character. Emphasise the significance of the main part, although do make sure that all children get their turn, if they want it. This is crucial, partly so that each child experiences being the central character and partly so that nobody feels excluded from a role that you are identifying as important.

What you need:

Narrative awareness - main character

Story props; paper, pen and clipboard for writing down children's suggestions; poster-sized paper; paints or drawing materials; marker pen for making poster; ready-made book for presenting children's ideas and drawings.

Extend this work into a painting and vocabulary activity. Make large posters with a painting of the central character and then discuss describing words with the children: 'The Very Hungry Caterpillar is green, squidgy, hungry, greedy, fat ...' Write down these suggestions on the poster or draft in any writers who are ready for the task, and then put up the poster in the book corner. If the activity grabs the children, repeat it with other stories to create a series of posters or a group book entitled 'Our favourite story characters'.

Choose books with a strong, recognisable and lovable central character such as David McKee's *Elmer the Elephant*, Gene Zion's *Harry the Dirty Dog* or Shirley Hughes' *Alfie*. One of the many advantages of these characters is that each one features in lots of books so that you can reinforce their importance with the interest of a new story.

As stories become more complex, so the number of significant characters increase. As you will generally be reading these stories with older ones, discuss with the children who they think is the most important person in the story. This can lead to some interesting debates: who is the most important character in Pat Hutchins' *Rosie's Walk*, Rosie or the fox? Who is central to Judith Kerr's *The Tiger Who Came to Tea*? Bear in mind that opinion will come into play here - most of us may think that Janet and Alan Ahlberg's Burglar Bill himself is the most important person in his story, but the child has a perfect right to decide that it is the baby. A story will always be what each individual makes of it, particularly where children are concerned.

Story endings:

All good stories must come to a close. This is partly what defines them as stories. Look out for strong, satisfying and comforting endings. For example, in *Mr Gumpy's Outing*, all the animals go home with Mr Gumpy and the children for tea. In *The Tiger Who Came to Tea* the story ends with the little girl and her family going to a cafe for dinner, since the tiger has eaten them out of house and home! Burglar Bill and Burglar Betty get married and give up their life of crime while Rosie (*Rosie's Walk*) gets safely home in time for dinner.

Help the children to focus on the conclusion of the story by discussing the possibility of a different ending. What might Burglar Bill and Burglar Betty have done instead of getting married? Ask a small group to think of a different ending and act it out. If you feel they need support, join in and take one of the roles yourself.

Relate the proposed ending to the child's own experience. For example, ask each child which cafe they would have chosen for dinner if the tiger had eaten all the food in their house.

What would their mummy or daddy have done or said after the tiger had gone?

Write down suggestions from each child and create a collection of different endings for a favourite story. Introduce your collection in some way, for example: 'At the end of *Mr Gumpy's Outing*, Mr Gumpy and the animals all go home to have tea. We have thought of some different endings. Jamie thinks that they all go to the fair. The sheep goes on the roundabout and the children go on the dodgems and they have candy floss. Then they go to bed. Annie thinks they have a picnic. They eat sandwiches and jelly. Then Mr Gumpy says goodbye.'

The children could produce drawings or paintings to accompany their endings. Make the endings into a big book, to hang on a hook in the book corner so that the children can look at and explore the different possibilities whenever they want to.

Other possibilities

Event sequences, the main character and endings are three of the most significant and accessible story elements for young children. You could try introducing other possibilities if you have older children with lots of story experiences and interest in books. For example, you could look at the dialogue in a book. Choose stories with clear, recognisable dialogue, such as *Mr Gumpy's Outing,* and take the opportunity to point out the speech marks. Or you could talk about settings. Look out for books with a well-defined landscape background in the pictures, such as the Ahlbergs' *Each Peach, Pear, Plum,* which takes place in the unmistakably English countryside, or Ezra Jack Keats' *Peter* stories, set in urban New York.

Activities of this kind are great fun and a good way of helping one of the more subtle, but nevertheless essential aspects of the child's literacy development. Reading means much more than simply being able to decode the words. If you can help a child develop an appreciation of stories, it will stay with her for life: literacy in the fullest sense of the word!

Assessment

In a large group, look out for signs that the child is concentrating on the story. Is she sitting quietly? Does she appear to be listening? Is she studying the pictures? Remember that 'sitting still' does not automatically mean that the child is absorbing the story. You may find that you can notice more if you observe the children when someone else is reading to them.

It is often easier to assess the child's understanding of story in an individual or small group session. Questions, comments and story-based discussion will help you judge her level of understanding. Reading the same book a number of times will enable you to assess how well the child remembers the story. Take note of questions and comments as these can show you how the child's understanding is developing from one reading to the next. Specific questions from you of the 'What do you think happens next?' variety can also be useful.

Books

Books with a strong sequence of events:

Mrs Mopple's Washing Line Anita Hewitt (Red Fox) ISBN 0 09 914411 5

The Very Hungry Caterpillar Eric Carle (Puffin) ISBN 0 14 05 0642 X

Mr Gumpy's Outing John Burningham (Puffin) ISBN 0 14 05 0254 8

Rosie's Walk Pat Hutchins (Puffin) ISBN 0 901223 71 X

The Gigantic Turnip (classic sequence tale originating from Russia) Aleksei Tolstoy, illustrations Niamh Sharkey (Barefoot Books) ISBN 1 902283 11 2

Brown Bear, Brown Bear, What Do You See? Bill Martin Jr/Eric Carle (Puffin) ISBN 0 14 05 0296 3

Well-known books with a strong and easily identifiable central character and good clear endings:

Mr Gumpy's Outing (see above)

Harry the Dirty Dog (and others in the series) Gene Zion (Red Fox) ISBN 0 09 972601 7

Titch (and others in the series) Pat Hutchins (Red Fox) ISBN 0 09 926253 3

Elmer (and others in the series) David McKee (Red Fox) ISBN 0 09 969720 3

The Very Hungry Caterpillar (see above)

Characters who have been featured on TV are also useful for focusing on central characters because they are familiar and recognisable. For example, Postman Pat, Fireman Sam, Noddy, Thomas the Tank Engine and Spot. Egmont Children's Books publish a wide range of character related books.

Word games

These activities introduce the child to new words through games and play experiences. Each has the potential to help the child towards the Early Learning Goal of 'extend(ing) vocabulary, exploring the meanings and sounds of new words.' Together, the activities have a particular value in relation to exploring meanings because they give concrete and active experience of the function of different word types - nouns, verbs, adjectives, adverbs and prepositions.

This is not as serious as it sounds. We are not teaching grammar and terms such as noun or verb are never mentioned. The aim is to provide the child with an active experience of the way in which a word type works. For example, in the action game (below), the child is given a number of action words to perform so that she experiences this group of words as something you *do*.

This approach aims to lay a foundation for future language study. The idea is that when the child learns about different types of words, much later in her schooling, she has some early concrete experiences to which she can tie the word group definitions.

Some of the games can be played with groups, some with pairs or individuals. They can be planned as set activities or, in many cases, played on the spur of the moment. Most important, they are active and great fun.

Naming objects (nouns)

This is a straightforward activity that can be started with the youngest

> **What you need:**
>
> **Naming objects**
>
> **Reading activity:** Object names written on cards.
>
> **Writing activity:** Slips of paper, pencil.

children in your setting. Simply point at objects and give their names, encouraging the children to join in and name the objects themselves.

The activity appeals to the young child's fascination for new words, particularly the names of things. It also offers the opportunity to introduce new words in the context of the object being named. If the child learns the name of something in its setting, it is more meaningful to her and more likely that she will retain the word. Practically, it helps the child feel at home. If you can name your surroundings, it increases your sense of belonging.

The activity can be done in a number of different ways. It can be a planned group activity - preferably a small rather than a large group. You can name small, portable objects, or you can take the children for a ramble around your setting, naming things as you go. It is usually most effective when done spontaneously - for example, a child or small group are gathered around you and showing interest in the tree in the garden. This is a good moment to do a little off-the-cuff activity and name the parts of the tree (branch, twig, leaf, trunk, and so on). Seizing the

moment in this way is ideal as you are following the interests of the children.

As well as naming single objects, you should aim to name the parts of an object. This helps the child focus on details and create a mental map of her environment - for example, branch, trunk, twig and leaf all go together because they are all parts of a tree.

The nature of the objects that you cover can be varied according to the age, developmental level and interests of the child or group. With some older ones you can get quite technical and detailed. The vehicle lover will enjoy working through the parts of a car (if possible, take a small group out to your car - much more exciting than pictures). The animal lover will be fascinated to learn the names for the different parts of the fish in the tank, or the gerbil in its

cage. There is great fun to be had trying to spot the fin before the fish darts behind a rock. And if the session develops into a discussion on why fish have fins, so much the better!

Reading activity

For those with reading skills, the game can develop into a reading and labelling activity if you choose simple words. Give the child ready written names to read and then place on the appropriate object. The context of the familiar setting, the previous oral work and the objects themselves will support her in reading the word successfully.

Writing activity

For those with writing skills, the child can write the name of an object on a ready prepared slip and place it on or beside the object itself.

Recording

If you have the time and the inclination, you can keep notes of what objects you have named with the children. A planned 'naming the parts of the tree' activity is easily recorded. Similarly, a spontaneous garden activity such as naming all the garden toys is easy to remember and make a note of. You can then follow up the activity with a little game, the next time you are in the garden: 'Who can remember what this is called?' Individual activities are less easy to record. For example, those occasions when you are in the toilet with a child and on the spur of the moment name the basin, the tap and the plug. Don't worry too much about trying to make a note of every new word you introduce or what the child has remembered. Children have a habit of absorbing and evolving language, whether we record it or not!

Some useful objects and parts to name with young children include: parts of a room (floor, wall, ceiling, window, door); parts of a door (handle, hinge, lock); parts of the body, parts of the

hand, foot, face; parts of a flower; parts of a book; parts of a chair; different papers and objects in the writing corner; objects in the home corner; objects linked to the painting easel; garden toys; objects in the toilet; parts of the toilet and sink.

The action game (verbs)

In this activity, the child is given an action word to perform: 'Pindar, will you *run*?', 'Tom, can you *crawl*?'. Emphasise the action word itself with the expression of your voice. In following these instructions, the child experiences each word as something that you do. Vary the action word according to the age group and developmental level of each child. Very little ones can walk, or jump, although you do need to give clear instructions as to where, along with a demonstration: '*Walk* to that chair and then back to the group.' Older children can also perform a simple action word, to show others what to do.

What you need:

Action game 1

Reading activity: Action words written on cards

Challenging action words for older ones include 'smile' or 'glance' or 'glare' - still something you do, but subtle. Put the action in a context, to help the child understand the meaning. For example, you could say: 'When my dog is naughty I *glare* at him, like this ...' You can also extend interest by introducing similes: 'Can you *crawl* like a baby?' or 'Can you *crawl* like a cat through the long grass?'

Depending on how long the activity holds the interest of your group, it can either be slipped into a couple of minutes at the beginning or end of a session, or extended into a longer group activity. It is also a good game to play spontaneously in the garden at playtime.

Reading activity

If you have children who are starting to read, extend this into a reading activity. There are many advantages to doing this: action words can easily be graded from the very simplest, such as 'run', 'hop', 'skip', to the very challenging, such as 'glance' or 'whisper'. This makes it an activity that you can use across the ability range, with something to stretch even the occasional fluent reader. The child also has to use her reading skills. Understanding what you read is the whole point of reading.

With this activity, the child has to interpret what she has read in order to perform the action. Both you and the child know she has read correctly by whether or not she can go on to do what it says on her card.

You can either write words for each child in the group, or use prepared cards so those who are ready can do it with minimal adult involvement. It is a lovely activity for the garden with space to make the most of the actions, and particularly good for the bouncers and wrigglers! If you have readers and non-readers in your group, simply give written instructions to the former and oral instructions to the latter.

The action game 2 (adverbs)

This is an extension of the first action game, to be introduced when the child has played action game 1 a few times. The child is given an adverb as well as a verb. For example, ask the child to run; then ask her to run *fast*; then ask her to run *slowly*. Use your voice to emphasise the adverb and ask the children to perform the same action (run) with a pair of contrasting adverbs (fast and slowly). This highlights that the words fast and slowly tell you how to perform the action.

Some action words:			
run	stand	yawn	hop
wink	laugh	rip	think
dance	sit	blink	glance
tap	drink	glare	hug
groan	skip	moan	jump
sing	grin	drag	spin

As with action game 1, vary the adverbs you use according to the age and ability of each child. A number of adverbs will be new to the children so

you do need to be ready to demonstrate them yourself.

Some adverbs:
fast/quickly/slowly
quietly/noisily/loudly
happily/sadly/crossly
clumsily/roughly/daintily/gently
neatly/messily

The farm game (adjectives)

The purpose of this game is to introduce words from the adjective group. The activity also gives the child experience of the fact that certain words distinguish one object from another, even if the objects fall within the same category. So, for example, we know that 'the *spotted* pig' is different from 'the *pink* pig' because of the two adjectives, *spotted* and *pink*.

You can use any kind of play set for this activity - a farmyard with a wide range of animals, a toy garage with lots of cars and other vehicles, a dolls' house with different chairs, beds and so on. Re-name the activity depending on what set you use, for example, the garage game or the dolls' house game. Use what you have available and try to pick something that will appeal to the child. The car-lover will be more receptive if you use the garage rather than the dolls' house, for example.

Taking the farmyard as an example, ask the child or small group to set it up and leave them to play with it for a while.

Join in at an appropriate moment and chat to the children about the animals. Bring the animals' 'qualities' into the conversation (the *black and white* cow, the *small* cow, the *brown* cow). Ask one of the children to place a cow in the barn. Then ask a child to put the *black and white* cow next to the cow in the

barn. Emphasise the adjective with your voice. Now ask a child to move the *small* cow into the yard. Suggest to the child that the *small* cow is lonely and can she put the *brown* cow with the *small* cow in the yard? Repeat with other groups of animals (the *pink* pig, the *spotted* pig, the *tiny* pig).

Through rearranging the groups of animals, the child experiences how a particular word tells her which cow or pig you are talking about.

Play games with the activity when the child is ready, to encourage her to use describing words herself: 'Can you guess which pig I am thinking of? .... No, I wasn't thinking of the *pink* pig, try again ......' Give some clues - 'The pig I'm thinking of is in the field - yes, you guessed right - I was thinking of the *spotted* pig.' Bear in mind that the child will often point to or give you the pig rather than describe it in words. Encourage her to use the language: if she points to a pig, ask her which one it is. If she cannot tell you, she is not yet ready for this part of the activity. Later, you can get the child using the language naturally by asking her to instruct you in rearranging the pigs, cows, sheep and so on.

Reading activity

If you have a child with advanced reading skills, this can be developed into a reading activity. Say to the child: 'I'm going to write down what I want you to give me.' You can then write 'the *pink* pig' for the child to read, highlighting the adjective by using a different colour. The context of the pigs and the fact that this follows on from lots of oral work will help the child read what has been written.

Other objects

You can do this activity with any group of objects from one category as long as each object has a distinguishing feature: shells, leaves, flowers, cars. You can also use the activity to introduce specific types of adjectives such as colour, shape or texture.

The play set does have some advantages over a group of objects, however. The child has the fun of playing with it; it is much easier for you and the child to chat about and it provides a more meaningful context - always useful when it comes to making sense of and absorbing new information.

The 'Where does it go?' game (prepositions)

The 'Where does it go?' game is similar to the farm game, but this time you and the child are using prepositions. Ask the child to put the cow *under* the tree, put the pig *beside* the cow, and so on. There are many prepositions you can draw from and introduce: by, with, around, above, below, outside, under, inside, across, over, through, within.

Don't be surprised to find that your children are unfamiliar with prepositions. Where this is the case, you will need to focus on just one word at a time: 'Can you put the pig *beside* the tree... Please move the farmer so he is *beside* the shed... I think the foal wants to be *beside* his mother.' Cater for a mixture of language abilities by using different prepositions with different children. You can also use a variety of words with the more able and just the one with the less able.

Once the child has grasped the general idea, you can start to exploit her enjoyment of 'nonsense' jokes by asking her to 'put the tree under the cow' as well as 'the cow under the tree'! This is a good activity for meeting the Scottish Curriculum Framework advice that children should 'have fun with language'. You can also switch roles, as in the farm game, with the child using prepositions by instructing you to rearrange the animals.

Apart from the fun of playing the game and coming across new words in context, the activity gives the child concrete experience of prepositions as words that change the position of one thing in relation to another.

Books

Naming and describing words

1001 Words Jan Pienkowski (Mammoth) ISBN 0 7497 2840 X

The Baby's Catalogue Janet and Alan Ahlberg (Puffin) ISBN 0 14 05 0385 4

Animals, Animals All Around Catherine and Laurence Anholt (Mammoth) ISBN 0 7497 3024 2

Action words

Look What I Can Do Catherine and Laurence Anholt (Mammoth) ISBN 0 7497 3423 X

Bouncing Shirley Hughes (Walker) ISBN 0 7445 3652 9

Snap Like a Crocodile! Kate Burns (Wayland) ISBN 1 899607 40 4
Blink Like an Owl! ISBN 1 899607 41 2
Waddle Like a Duck! ISBN 1 899607 42 0
Jump Like a Frog! ISBN 1 899607 35 8

Position words

Rosie's Walk Pat Hutchins (Puffin) ISBN 0 14 050032 4

Where's the Cat? Stella Blackstone (Barefoot Books) ISBN 1 901223 71 X

Reading activity

Extend this into a reading activity in the same way as the farm game. Write the instruction, highlighting the preposition in a different colour.

This is a challenging reading activity, to be kept up your sleeve for the occasional advanced reader.

News time

News time is one of the most popular language based activities in the early years setting - and with good reason. It provides an excellent forum for speaking and listening within a group, making it a useful activity in helping the children towards the Early Learning Goal of 'speak(ing) clearly and audibly with confidence and control'. The child's confidence is helped by the fact that the subject matter is her own news and thus, something she is familiar with. Because she is drawing from her own experiences, the activity also meets the speaking and listening goals of 'us(ing) language to imagine and recreate roles and experiences' and 'us(ing) talk to organise, sequence and clarify thinking, ideas, feelings and events.'

Although news time revolves around speaking, it is equally useful as a listening activity, with the potential to help the child towards the goal of 'sustain(ing) attentive listening'.

The news time activity

This activity is flexible and open-ended. The principle is straightforward - simply gather together a group and invite each child to tell their news. There are, however, a number of group management issues to bear in mind in order to help the children get as much as possible from the activity.

A good starting point is to tell your own news and inform the children that each one of them will also have a turn if they have any news they would like to tell the group. You may need to give some suggestions: Did anyone go on an outing at the weekend? Did anyone have a visitor?

What age?

If possible, have a range of ages in your group. Younger ones learn so much from older ones, and it is good for the older ones to have the chance to be patient and supportive to the little ones who are not experienced at speaking before a group. Once the older ones have got the idea, they can be useful in showing the younger or less confident children how to go about giving their news.

Managing the group

Help the children to 'sustain attentive listening' by providing a good role model as a listener. Give the speaker all your attention, while at the same time remaining constantly aware of the state and mood of the group. Remember that you can only expect so much from young listeners. Little ones are not always the most compelling speakers so it is up to you to do whatever you can to make news time as good an experience for both listener and speaker as possible.

For example, be ready to prompt the child who dries up. This is important if you are going to maintain the dignity of the speaker and hold the attention of the rest of the group. If the speaker doesn't manage to recover and carry on, help her to finish off on a positive note.

Gently cut short the 'rambler'. Some children want to finish but don't know how. Others want to steal the show and need to realise that they must share the stage. If you have a child who desperately wants to communicate beyond her fair share of the group time, promise that she can tell you later and make sure you keep your promise. Cutting a speaker short is not always easy to do in a positive way; this is one method of helping the child feel that her communications are heard and valued, even if that means a one-to-one conversation later in the day.

Always keep your response positive and 'smiley'. Whatever the age of the speaker, it makes a huge difference to have someone in your audience who is evidently listening to you and enjoying what you have to say.

Assessment

Look out for the child's ability to communicate effectively to the group. This includes: speaking clearly and audibly; looking at the other children; showing objects so that everyone can see; a confident manner; whether or not the child is willing to stand up and is comfortable doing so.

The content of the child's news is also important: if appropriate, can she stick to the theme? How extensive is her vocabulary? How complex are her sentences? How well is she able to finish off?

Look out for the ability to listen and show courtesy towards the speaker - although you should always take into account whether or not the speaker is engaging!

Managing a news time group successfully takes all your concentration. It is usually easier to observe and make assessments when someone else is holding the group. Try to observe on a regular basis and take surreptitious notes for your records.

Sitting or standing?

Encourage the child to stand in order to tell her news. If a speaker stands, she is in a better position to gain and hold the attention of her audience. However, if you have a child who prefers to sit, be ready to accept that. Likewise, accept the child who prefers not to speak. Remember to invite her each time, but accept a refusal with equanimity. The best way of encouraging the reticent child is to help her feel comfortable and unpressurised. Even if a child never contributes her own news, she still plays a valuable role in the group by being one of the listeners.

When?

Monday morning is a good time for your news session as the children are fresh from weekend activities. It can also provide a link between home and school at the start of a new week. If you do hold the activity on a regular day and time, watch out for it becoming a bit stale and routine. You could vary the time or format a little; concentrate on a common theme, such as birthdays, to encourage the children to use their memories.

Something to show

Ask the children if they would like to bring in an object to talk about (although watch that this doesn't turn into a 'bring and brag' session with your older ones). If a child wants to talk about a weekend or holiday trip, encourage her to bring in a related object, such as a photograph, postcard, brochure, guide book or souvenir. This is useful in prompting the child and interesting for the others to look at. Start helping the children learn how to show something so that everybody can see clearly - carrying it around the semi-circle, holding it up high. This contributes to the Early

Learning Goal of 'show(ing) awareness of the listener'.

Arranging your group

The physical organisation of the children depends on the personality of the group. In some ways, this is a serious activity that suits a more formal setting. A semi-circle of chairs enables all children to see the speaker and also cuts down on the opportunity for members of the audience to distract each other! Alternatively, you may feel that a relaxed group on the carpet makes it less daunting for young speakers. You could explore both approaches to see which works best.

Dictation

Dictation in the early years setting consists of the child telling you her stories, poems, letters, messages and thoughts so that you can write them down on her behalf. The child takes great delight in the fact that you will write down what she says, and the activity has the potential to make some important contributions to literacy development. For instance, it helps to introduce the act of writing and reinforces the idea that written words are symbols for spoken words. It can contribute to the Welsh Desirable Learning Outcome that children should 'understand some of the functions of writing'. It also shows the link between reading and writing as you write down the child's thoughts and then read them back to her.

What age?

This activity is simple, versatile and flexible. It can be done with an individual, a small group or a large group. Depending on the age of the child, her developmental level and the purpose of the written communication, the dictation may take only a few moments, or it may extend over a long period of time. You and the child may produce reams of writing or just a few simple words.

Talking about pictures

Invite a child to tell you about her painting and write down what she says on the picture itself. This is a good opportunity because it keeps the activity related to the child - *her* painting, *her* thoughts and words. It is useful in helping parents see that their child's picture is special and has a meaning.

Try to avoid asking the child what she has painted or drawn. The picture may not yet represent anything in the child's mind, in which case the question will only confuse her. Keep your questions open-ended and if the child is unresponsive, leave this activity until she is a little older.

Written communications

The young child needs to realise that writing is a means of communicating her thoughts and ideas to another person. The concept of 'the reader' is abstract and difficult for her to grasp, particularly as her understanding of reading is still at the developmental stage. One of the best ways of introducing the communicative possibilities in writing is for the child to dictate a note or message to an individual she knows and can envisage. Dictating a message for Mummy who can then read it later provides a powerful way of getting across the purpose of writing. She can even dictate a note to remind herself to take something home. The fact that she won't be able to read the note in the traditional sense doesn't matter - she will remember the content and purpose of the written words, giving her a positive and meaningful experience of the whole process.

Apart from dictating messages the child can also write to friends at home and at school, other adults in the setting, neighbours and relatives. To begin with, you may need to encourage the children by asking them to whom they would like to send a message, letter or card. You may also need to

prompt them and discuss the content of their message. Look out for opportunities that crop up throughout the session - a get-well card for Granny, a message to a helper asking if she will read a particular story at home time.

As the children start to realise the purpose of writing, they will come up with occasions when they want to write. You can then become less of an instigator and more of a facilitator.

Use a variety of different writing papers, cards and note papers. For example, if you have a group dictating a letter to a poorly child or a thank-you letter following a trip, discuss with the children the appropriate paper to use.

Themes and topics

Dictation is useful if you are looking at a particular topic or theme with your children. Lists, poems, stories, sentences to explain a picture, annotated drawings and labels are all writing forms that can be used to present information. Providing these opportunities will help your children towards the Early Learning Goal of 'attempt(ing) writing for various purposes, using features of different forms such as lists, stories, instructions'. You may find that some older ones can help you plan your topic or theme. Write down their ideas and suggestions, so that they can be involved in the topic from the very beginning.

In the case of titles, annotations or naming the parts of a picture, write what the child wants to say on sticky labels so that she can either add them to the picture by herself or play a major part in the process, depending on what she is ready for.

Signs and notices

Look out for any possible opportunity for writing: menus for snack time, labels and notices, sets of instructions. These could include a reminder for children to wash their hands after going to the toilet, a list of the things kept in a particular drawer or a notice for parents. All of these messages have to be constructed; the right words have to be chosen and the writer has to think about whether the content of her writing makes sense and expresses what she wants to say. Encourage the children to come up with ideas and discuss the different ways that something could be said. Read back to them what they have dictated so they can decide whether or not they are happy with the end result.

Stories

Children who have listened to lots of stories are capable of making up their own stories from as young as two years. There are a number of purposes to storytelling. Children use narrative to make sense of situations and events, explore moral issues such as good and bad, play with words and language and explore their established view of life by turning it upside down. It is a natural and fun activity that we should tap into to help the child's literacy development.

Apart from sharing good books with the children, it is also important that the adults in the setting tell stories - little narratives based on your own experiences, retelling a favourite tale from a book or appropriate fairy stories. Choose the latter carefully for little ones - remember that some are more suitable for older children. You can then encourage the children to create their own stories, either individually or in

groups, with you writing down their thoughts and ideas as they go along.

You may need to help the child with the planning and structure of the story. Who are the characters? Where is it happening? How is it going to begin? Be ready to prompt the child with 'Once upon a time...' type openings. Although some teachers often try to steer older children away from these conventions, they make useful tools for the little one who is still getting to grips with basic story structures. Once started, the story will probably take off, although you may need to help with an ending. As you write, you could make subtle changes to grammar, but stay as faithful to the child's original thoughts as possible.

After you have written down each part, read it back to the child and ask her if she is happy with it. Alternatively, you can avoid interrupting her narrative flow and read the whole story back to her when she has finished. Discuss the possibility of making changes to the story. This activity of dictating and then revising your work shows the child that writing is a creative process, as well as an end result. It also has a part to play in helping the child progress towards the Early Learning Goals of 'retell(ing) narratives in the correct sequence, drawing on the language patterns of stories' and 'us(ing) language to imagine and recreate roles and experiences'.

As part of the child's information technology learning, make tape recorders available. The children can then record their stories independently for you to transcribe.

Watch out for the children becoming too dependent on you doing the writing. While dictation is an invaluable means of enabling the child to record her thoughts at an early

stage, ultimately you want to ease the child into writing for herself. If some of your children are ready to start writing, encourage and support their attempts as much as you can.

Assessment

Dictation is a means to an end. The early stages simply involve getting across to the child the idea that you can write down her words. Look out for the point at which the child starts asking you to write for her. This shows that she is beginning to grasp the purpose of writing.

Talking about pictures, Written communications, Themes and topics, Signs and notices and **Stories** - look out for how clearly the child can express herself and how well her speech fits the purpose of the writing. For example, do her words relate to her painting? Does her note to Mummy say what she wants it to? What contribution does she make to a group story? Bear in mind the factors that will influence the child's abilities - age, special needs, home experience, English as a second language. Look out also for the child starting to write for herself, regardless of her skills in this area. This shows that she is developing a real sense of herself as a writer.

Language and **Literacy**

I spy with a difference

This activity provides good preparation for both reading and writing. It is based on the format of the well loved 'I spy' game and its purpose is to help the child recognise the separate sounds that constitute a word. This makes it a useful contribution to the Early Learning Goal of being able to 'hear and say initial and final sounds in words, and short vowel sounds within words'. As a game that encourages the child to explore and play with words and their sounds, it is also useful in meeting the Scottish Curriculum Framework advice that children should 'develop an awareness of letter names and sounds in the context of play experiences'.

The game follows a number of stages, taking the child from the youngest age in an early years setting to the reception year and beyond. The child should be allowed to progress at her own pace through the stages. **The ages given for each stage are to be regarded as broad guidelines only. As always with the young child, it is far more important to gauge what she is ready for, rather than follow a strict progression based solely on chronological age.**

Phase one
(two and a half years onwards)

Gather together a number of familiar, everyday objects. Hold an object in your hand, such as a book, and say to the children: 'I spy with my little eye something I am holding beginning with b. Unlike traditional 'I spy', you give the sound made by the letter b (buh) rather than its name (bee). The answer should be obvious to the

---

What you need:

Phases one and two

A selection of familiar, everyday objects beginning with different initial sounds. For example: egg, pen, cup, watch, nut, spoon, book, dog, fork, shoe, goat, mouse, rabbit, doll, orange, hat, table, zebra, umbrella, apple.

---

children. Unlike the usual 'I spy' this is not a guessing game. If a child does not grasp how to play the game after a few turns, she is not yet ready for it.

Repeat as often as possible with different objects and different sounds. Ring the changes - put a cup on the table and say: 'I spy with my little eye something on the table beginning with c ...' or 'I spy something I am wiggling beginning with f ...' (finger) or 'I spy something I am touching beginning with p ...' (pen).

At this very early stage, do not have more than one object in view so there can be no room for confusion. Make sure you choose objects that the children can name easily - for example, a cassette for c may fox a number of children, even though most will have come across the object itself. Avoid objects with two common names, such as chicken and hen. If you spy something beginning with h and the child says 'chicken', it does not help her to grasp the idea of listening for the initial sound in a word.

Play the game as much as possible, introducing a wide variety of objects/sounds and varying your questions and challenges to maintain the child's interest.

Phase two
(around three years onwards)

Once you feel the children are starting to listen to the sounds (this could take a few weeks), move on to having two objects on the table at one time, for example, a doll and a cup. Now the children have to choose which object you are spying by listening to the sound and associating it with the name of one of the objects on the table. Repeat this and gradually build up the number of objects to five or six, for example, a pencil, a horse, a car, an elephant and a flower.

When you reach this stage, it is easy to assess whether a child has grasped the skill of recognising the initial sound of a word by whether she can play the game successfully. If she persistently fails to choose the appropriate object, she is not ready and you can simply go back to phase one. If necessary, you can combine phases one and two for different children within the same session. Have your collection of objects on the table, pick up one of them and say: 'Connor, I spy something I am holding beginning with p ....' Then, for the child who is ready for the greater challenge, you can leave all the objects on the table and say: 'Sushma, I spy something on the table beginning with r ....'

To begin with, avoid having two objects with similar initial sounds on the table ('pen' and 'ball' for example, or 'van' and 'whistle'). As the child's ear becomes more and more attuned to the different sounds, you can start to introduce pairs of objects such as these.

Gradually increase the challenge of the game. Choose a part of the room - 'I spy something beginning with c in the book corner' (cushion). Or use yourself - 'I spy something I am wearing beginning with s (socks). Introduce the point that several different words begin with the same sound. 'Can you spy anything else I am wearing beginning with s?' (scarf, skirt, sandals) You can then have great fun surreptitiously pointing to your sandals if the children need a bit of help!

If necessary, plant things in the room. For example, 'I spy something near the home corner beginning with p'; the child might offer 'piano', but your group can then go on to spot the plant, the pot, the paint, pencils and paper that you placed near the piano before you began the activity. Remember that this is 'I spy with a difference'. The child doesn't have to guess the object you were thinking of. Any object beginning with that sound will do!

One or two children may be ready to do the 'I spy ...' themselves, asking you and the other children to guess what they have spied. At this stage you are playing the game similarly to the usual format although the emphasis is on sound, not spelling. Traditionally you

might say 'I spy something beginning with 'gee' ' (giraffe). However, in this version, we would say: 'I spy something beginning with j' ('juh') because giraffe begins with the *sound* j, even though it is spelt with a g.

Phase three
(around four years, depending on how much experience child has had of phases one and two)

Once the child is adept at identifying the initial sound in a word, you can move on to listening for the final sound in a word. This comes quite

---

What you need:
Phase three

A selection of familiar, everyday objects beginning with the same sound but ending in a different sound. For example:

pig, pen, puppet

cup, coat, clock

ball, book, boat

---

easily to the child who is ready and when she hears a final sound for the first time, it often gives her more of a kick than listening for initial sounds.

Return to using just two or three carefully chosen objects. This time they must all begin with the same sound but have a different final sound. For example, pen, pig and puppet. Play the game as follows: 'I spy with my little eye, something beginning with p and ending with g'. This time, the challenge is to listen for the end sound. If the child gives the wrong answer, respond positively - 'Yes, pen begins with p but I am spying something beginning with p and ending with g'. Let's listen to the last sound in 'pen'. You can then work through all the objects until you get to the word that ends with g - 'pig'.

If the child has persistent difficulty, she is not ready. Simply go back to phase two. 'I spy' is such a universally popular activity, with so much opportunity for variety, there is little danger of her getting bored until she is ready for this new phase.

Phase four
(around four to four and a half years onwards)

In order to read and write, the child needs to be able to analyse all the sounds that make up a word. The previous phases of the game have been preparing for and working towards this goal.

Choose a simple word that you have used in the previous stages, such as 'cup'. Ask the child to identify the first and last sounds in 'cup' - c and p - and then explain that you are now going to

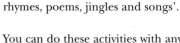

What you need:

Rhyme games

Sets of two or three pictures with names that rhyme. For example:

head, bed, red

car, star, jar

chair, hair, bear

hen, pen, ten

say all the sounds in 'cup' - c-u-p. Continue with other words, gradually choosing longer and longer words to sound out as your children become ready. You can cater for different abilities within the same group by giving less or more challenging words to the children to sound out. By this stage you don't need the 'I spy ...'

Remember that it is sound, not spelling, that you are concentrating on and that you are breaking the words into the smallest units of sound (phonemes). So, the word 'house' is sounded out as 'h-ou-s' rather than 'h-o-u-s-e'. The word 'bottle' is sounded out as 'b-o-t-l' rather than 'b-o-t-t-l-e'. Analysing how sounds make up words in this way does not affect later spelling as this is an oral, listening activity, not a visual, reading activity. Gradually, as the child is exposed to more and more written language, she will gather visual experience of how phonemes and words are spelt.

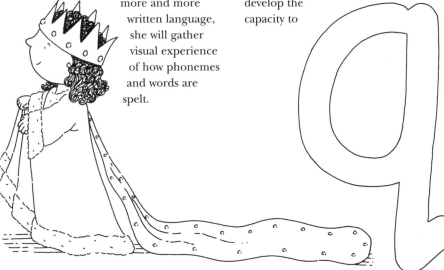

Bilingual children should be encouraged to play 'I spy with a difference' using the sounds in their home language, as well as English. Ask members of the child's family or community to come into school, or explain to the child's parents how to play it at home.

Extension work
Sound games and rhymes

Although 'I spy with a difference' is an enjoyable game, it is quite a structured means of introducing children to phonemic awareness (awareness of sound). The skill of phonemic awareness is so fundamental to both reading and writing that you cannot give the children too many opportunities to develop in this area. Nor can you have too great a variety of activities at your finger-tips.

The following games encourage the children to play with and explore sounds and rhymes. For settings in Scotland, they fit in with the Scottish Curriculum Framework advice that children should 'have fun with language' and 'listen and respond to the sounds and rhythm of words in...rhymes.' For settings in Northern Ireland, they contribute to the Pre-school Curricular Guidance that the children should have 'opportunities to listen to... rhymes' and develop the capacity to

'listen and respond to... nursery rhymes, poems, jingles and songs'.

You can do these activities with any size of group, or even with individual children. They can be planned in advance or slipped into a couple of spare minutes. The spur of the moment activity is often the most successful because there is less pressure on the children to 'perform' than is sometimes the case in the more formal group setting.

Games with names

Take each child's name and turn it into a nonsense rhyme by adding different initial sounds: Christopher, Bistopher, Mistopher; Hannah, Bannah, Spannah; Joe, Poe, Moe. Watch out for the new names you inadvertently create if a child is sensitive - Jessie might object to becoming Messie.

Sounds with rhymes

Play the 'I spy' game with rhymes: 'I spy something that rhymes with jug' (mug). If necessary, plant appropriate objects in the room, or have a selection of objects on the table.

Odd one out

Recite three words to the children and ask them to pick out the one that doesn't rhyme. For example: pig, big, pen; boat, coat, brick; cook, bed, book. This activity requires the children to have well developed listening skills.

Rhyme games

Cut out pictures from magazines to mount on cards or ask the artist in your setting (or a skilful mum or dad) to draw pictures of familiar objects for the children to group according to rhyme. For example, you could have a set of cards with pictures of the following: pen, hen, ten; rug, mug, jug; chair, hair, bear. Mix them up for the child then show her how to put them into their rhyme groups.

Another possibility is to slip one card into each group for the child to spot as the odd one out (pen, hen, chair and ten, for example). Have a number of sets so that the child can continue the activity by herself or in a small group. Gradually you can build up a wide collection, covering a huge range of rhymes.

Rhymes and jingles

Make up your own rhymes and jingles with the children. The following give the children plenty of direction as to the word to choose:

I'm thinking of a word that sounds like feet

When dinner time comes it's time' to ......

I'm thinking of a word that sounds like hat

I say miaow so I'm a ......

I'm thinking of a word that sounds like dig

I say oink, oink so I'm a ....

I'm thinking of a word that sounds like head

When I start to yawn I go to......

I'm thinking of a word that sounds like bell

Ding, dong, ding, dong, pussy's in the......

Using this format, these rhymes are relatively easy to make up yourself. While it is obvious to us what the rhyming word is meant to be, the purpose of the activity is sound recognition through rhyme. This means that you could accept any answer that rhymes and still maintain the aim of the child practising and

demonstrating sound awareness. Alternatively, you may want to stick to a jingle that makes sense on the basis that language is a meaningful mode of communication. If you go for this second approach, watch out for nonsense rhymes produced by the child in the full knowledge that they are nonsense. If the child comes up with 'I say miaow so I'm a bat' with lots of giggles, then she has clearly gone beyond the literal meaning and is playing with words/rhymes - a valuable learning activity in its own right!

The following rhymes give children plenty of freedom to think of different rhyming words:

I am a bee

And I live in .....

(a tree, a cup of tea)

On top of a hill

I saw ......

(a mill, Bill)

Sitting on a mat

I saw ......

(a cat, a hat)

Lying in bed

I saw ......

(a head, Fred)

With this set of jingles, it is a good idea to accept all answers as long as they rhyme. As well as being great fun, nonsense verse has the capacity to widen considerably the choice of rhyming words available to the children.

Look out for the creative opportunities in this activity. You may find that the children extend the activity beyond the limits of your jingle, to produce a rhyming poem.

Books

Rhyme

My Very First Mother Goose Iona Opie/Rosemary Wells (Walker) ISBN 0 7445 4400 9 Traditional nursery rhymes and jingles - great for helping children develop sound awareness.

Hairy Maclary from Donaldson's Dairy Linley Dodd (Puffin) ISBN 0 14 050531 8 Hilarious rhyming text that trips off the tongue!

Pass the Jam, Jim Kaye Umansky (Red Fox) ISBN 0 09 918571 7 Fun alliterative rhyming text and jolly illustrations.

If you want to try making your own sets of rhyming cards or write your own jingles, the following groups of words can be used as a starting point. Each group consists of everyday, familiar words. They are only a small sample of the rhyming words that crop up in the English language. If you want to think of further groups, all you need to do is look about the room/garden/shop/ street and you will find numerous words to start you off.

ball, hall, tall, fall, small, Paul
peg, leg, egg
feet, meet, eat, seat, Pete, sheet, treat
car, jar, star, far, bar
bee, sea, tea, tree, me, she, he, we, knee, pea, three
can, man, fan, van, Dan
hill, pill, Jill, Bill, fill, spill, mill, still
chair, stair, bear, share, fair
mat, cat, bat, sat, hat, rat, fat
run, bun, fun, sun
bed, head, Fred, said, red, shed, Ted
cow, ow, bow, now, how
chin, bin, tin, in, pin, thin, win

Feely letters

This activity relates to 'I spy with a difference' (see page 38) and helps the child to progress towards the Early Learning Goals of 'link(ing) sounds to letters, naming and sounding the letters of the alphabet' and 'form(ing) recognisable letters, most of which are correctly formed'. The play elements in both the main activity and the extension activities help to meet the Scottish Curriculum Framework advice that children should 'develop an awareness of letter names and sounds in the context of play experiences.'

What age?

If you play 'I spy' with your group, the child should be ready to start matching sounds and letters when she can recognise the initial sound of a word and is familiar with the fact that many words can begin with the same sound (Phase two of 'I spy').

Making feely letters

You need either to buy or make a set of letters that are tactile in some way so that the child can feel the shape of a letter as well as look at it. Trace round letter templates onto the back of sandpaper, velvet, furry material, felt or any other substance you wish to use. Cut them out and stick them onto cards or wooden plaques. Place the letter either to the right of the plaque so there is a space for the right-handed child to place the left hand on the plaque to steady it, or in the centre to make it easy for both left- and right-handed children to use. It can also be useful to put a line under the letter, to remind the children which way up the letter goes, and a dot at the point where you start to feel/write the letter. (When you draw round the letters, remember to place them back to front on the material. This will ensure that they are the right way round when you cut them out.)

Give a little thought to the script you choose. Research now shows that children learn to read perfectly well whether exposed to a cursive form (**a not a, g not g**) of letters or not because they are so used to seeing a variety of letter styles in the printed material around them. The advantage of starting with a cursive style is that it is smoother and more flowing, and lends itself much more easily to joining up when the child reaches that stage of

What you need:

Making feely letters

To make your own feely letters, you need:

■ tactile material, such as velvet, furry fabric, sandpaper or felt

■ chalk or felt pen

■ sharp scissors

■ strong glue

■ wooden or stiff cardboard plaques

■ black permanent ink marker pen for adding lines and dot

Introduce each letter. 'This makes the sound d. What words can we think of that begin with the sound d?'

Feel the letter with the index and middle finger of the writing hand, in the way that it is written. At the same time as feeling the letter, say its sound.

Invite each child in the group to have a go, reminding them of the sound the letter makes and encouraging them to say it and feel it.

Repeat this as often as you feel it is necessary for the child to learn to link the sound with the symbol, watching out to ensure that you are keeping the group's interest.

Phase two

Give the children lots of practice with identifying and finding the letters. Ask questions and set little challenges: 'Jade, can you give me the letter g?' When the child does so, encourage her to feel it as it is written and repeat its sound, to help her fix both symbol and sound in her memory.

Ring the changes with your questions and move the letters about from time to time:

'Can you put the letter a next to the letter g?'

'Put the letter g under your chair.'

'Balance the letter d on your knee.'

You may prefer shorter, snappier instructions - 'Touch d', 'Move g', 'Where's a?', 'Feel g'. You may wish to make it more active, depending on the personality of your little group: 'Can you hide a in the book corner for Jade to find?' As long as you stick to the aim, bring your own approach and ideas to this part of the activity.

---

her writing development. In other words, it avoids learning one set of letters at the pre-school stage and a completely new set when you come to do joined-up handwriting later. However, it is up to each individual setting. If you are unsure, contact the schools that you 'feed' to ask them what script they use and what they would find a helpful preparation.

The letters you use do not have to be textured and the child does not have to trace them with the fingers. Feely letters do, however, help to prepare the child's hand for writing the letter through feeling as well as seeing its shape.

Linking sound and symbol

Once you have your set of feely letters, you are ready to show the child the link between sound and symbol. Introduce the activity to a single child or small group. Try not to have more than three children in your group although, as always, this will depend on your time, resources, your adult/child ratio and the number of children who are ready for the activity.

When introducing the child to the letters, it is useful to follow a three phase process. Phase one introduces the activity, making the initial link and showing the child what you are going to be doing. Phase two gives the child lots of practice and experience, helping to establish this new information. Phase three is where you discover whether the child has learned and can remember and use the new information.

It is important that each phase remains fun and light hearted, particularly phase three. If the child feels tested or pressurised in any way, she will cease to enjoy herself which, in turn, will affect her learning. Remember also that young children vary enormously in their readiness for this kind of learning. Do not push those who struggle with letters and sounds. Simply leave the activity for when they are older - which may even be when they have moved on to the next stage of their schooling.

Phase one

To start off, choose three letters that contrast in both letter shape and sound (for example, a, d and g rather than b, p and q.)

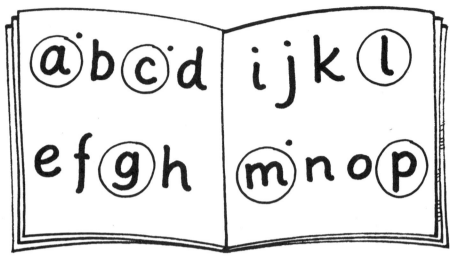

Phase three

This is the final phase where you find out how well the children can attach the sound to its letter. This time you don't mention the name of the letter. Point to one of the letters and ask: 'Jade, what sound does this make? Can you feel it?' If the child doesn't know, simply go back to phase two activities (the child won't realise that you are going back a phase so there is no danger of her feeling that she has failed). If you are doing this activity with a group, and you find that one child isn't ready for phase three, simply continue asking her phase two questions while you carry out phase three with the others.

Recording

For keeping records, issue each child with his or her own little letter booklet. Encourage the children to decorate their booklets and write the child's name on the front cover. Write each letter inside the booklet so that the child can circle the letters they have worked with. You can keep your own notes of their progress and when you feel that they actually know the letter, you can add a little dot or some other mark as a sign that they have not only worked with that letter but they have learned it.

Progress through all the letters in the alphabet in this way. Once the first session has been completed, try to include one letter from a previous session in the next. For example, if session one consisted of a, d and g, session two could be a, c and f.

Do as much follow-up work as possible to help fix the letters in the child's mind. Don't assume that one successful session working through the three phases will result in the child retaining the letter. This may be the case with some children but the majority need lots of further activities. The following games and ideas are all active and enjoyable ways of consolidating this special new knowledge.

Hunt the letter

Write different letters on pieces of paper to hide around the room. Give each child a feely letter and send them off to search for the matching letter.

What you need:
Hunt the letter

A set of feely letters

The letters of the alphabet written on separate slips or cards

---

Hide letters in the room. Give each child a letter sound and ask the children to search for the letter that matches their sound: 'Can you find the letter that says p?' Hide several letters so those who find their letter quickly can go on to look for more. Make a list of the hidden letters and tick them off as they are brought to you so that you don't despatch a child to search for a letter that has already been found.

Checking letters

Slip in little checking activities at odd moments. Spend a couple of minutes with the letters after register, before snack time, lunch time or story time. This can be invaluable, yet it takes up little space in your day and requires virtually no planning. Simply hold up a letter and ask the children to say its sound. If you have the whole group together, there is the advantage of sparking interest and offering an experience for a younger child to absorb. It is surprising how much little ones will take in without you even realising.

Letters in books

Encourage a child to search for letters she can recognise when looking at a book. A selection of good alphabet books is particularly useful for this activity.

Letters and objects

Gather together objects whose names begin with the initial letters you and your children have covered. Place them in a basket or box and select the matching feely letters. Hold up a letter and ask the children to give you its sound. Next ask a child to find an object in the box that begins with that sound and place it next to the letter on the mat.

If you have a group who need to move around, give each child a letter, ask the children to identify its sound and then

What you need:

Letters and objects

A set of feely letters

A basket of familiar, everyday objects with clear initial sounds, such as : cup, dog, cat, flower, pencil, sweet, peg, book, lemon, rubber, elephant, watch, horse, donkey, chair, ring.

despatch them around the setting searching for an object beginning with that sound. You may need to plant appropriate objects in the room and direct the child to a certain area: 'Find something beginning with your feely letter in the book corner'.

Ask the children to bring their objects to you to place beside their letters. Gather the group together at the end of the activity and go through what each child has found as a further reinforcement.

As well as working through the sounds and symbols of the 26 letters in the alphabet, you can also include common digraphs (two letters that make a new sound when put together). English is a non-phonetic language, which means that there are more sounds in the language than letters to represent them. It is a particularly challenging language in its written form because different sounds are spelt in different ways. For example, the oa sound in boat can also be spelt with an oe as in toe, an o as in so, an ew as in sew, an ow as in low or an ough as in though. If the child has lots of experiences of meaningful, interesting literature through sharing good picture books with adults, she will build up a sight vocabulary of common digraphs, letter clusters and frequently recurring words. Along

with these broad experiences, there is also a value in introducing the child to some of the most common digraphs, for example, th, sh, ch, wh, ai as in train, ee as in sleep, oa as in loaf, ie as in tie, ar as in car, or as in for, and er as in her. You can either make these into feely letters, or simply write them onto cards to introduce to the children, following the three phases described above.

It is important to bear in mind that these activities relate to the mechanical element of reading. They can provide a useful contribution to the development of the child as a reader, but they should be seen as just one element in a much wider picture that includes the full range of literacy related activities.

Assessment

Look out for how well the child remembers the sound for each letter. Phase three of the activity will tell you that the child has learned the letter, but you do need to play lots of follow-up games to check whether she can remember it over a period of time. Only record the child as knowing the sound/symbol when she has shown that she has retained her new knowledge.

Feeling the letters (preparation for writing) - make a note of whether the child is starting at the top and tracing the letter with her index and middle fingers, as it is written. If the child can learn to feel the letter as it is written, it makes writing letters a more straightforward process - but don't make too big an issue of it at this early stage.

ACTIVITY

Listening games

Listening skills are vital to a child's language development, particularly when it comes to absorbing spoken language and developing as a conversationalist. There are many games the children can play to focus their attention on listening and help them refine this important sense. Many of them are suitable for a mixed age group, with the child responding to the activity at her own level. Many can be slipped into a spare couple of minutes, or planned as set activities. They can be done with one or two children at a time, with a small group or with a large group. Collectively, they help the children meet the Early Learning Goal requiring them to 'sustain attentive listening.' Most important of all, they are great fun!

Giraffes

The children pretend either to be giraffes (stretching up tall), owls (standing with arms by sides) or ants (curled up as small as possible on the floor). They have to listen carefully as the adult calls out one of the animal groups, and then respond with the appropriate movement, as quickly as possible.

Introduce variations, for example, kangaroos (the children do stand jumps with legs together), frogs (crouch jumps on the floor) and elephants (wave an arm as a trunk and plod slowly about).

Challenge the children further by lowering your voice so they have to keep very still and quiet and listen carefully. The children can also take turns to call out the animal.

Little echo

Gather a small group for this activity. One child is chosen to be Little Echo. The adult says a message and the child has to repeat it, a little more quietly if she is able. A further challenge is for the adult to whisper a message for the child to repeat (in a normal voice) to the group. Try to keep the interest of the children waiting for their turn by giving funny and entertaining messages. You and child can switch roles and the child can say or whisper a message to the adult. When you have reproduced it, check with the child that you have done so correctly.

What sound is it?

The children close their eyes and the adult makes a familiar and recognisable sound - clapping, coughing, yawning, sneezing, stamping. The children have to guess what the sound is. Don't ask new or anxious children to keep their eyes closed; it is only easy to do if you feel completely at home and relaxed in your environment. If the children can't resist peeking (as is often the case) go behind a screen such as a bookcase.

What you need:

What sound is it?

A screen/bookcase to hide behind

A variety of materials to make recognisable sounds, such as paper for tearing or musical instruments

As an extension - a tape recorder and tape of recorded sounds

---

Alternatively, make a tape recording. This lets you widen the variety of sounds. It can cause great amusement - a toilet flushing, for example.

Possibilities include laughter, tearing paper, the washing machine, someone whistling. You need to think carefully about what children of this age will have a chance of recognising. Also think about how specific you want to be. Will you accept 'music' or 'a song' for 'piano playing' or do you want the instrument? Is the piano played by someone in your setting? If so, your children can probably identify it, or are they unlikely to have come across the sound of a piano?

You can play this with a group of related sounds. For example, if the children have been working with percussion instruments, see if they can identify the instrument from sound alone.

Sound pairs

This is a game for one or two children to play together. Gather eight cylindrical, lidded containers - sweet tubes, empty film canisters, empty spice pots. Divide the pots into pairs and fill each pair with a substance such as macaroni, rice, chick peas or sand. Check that each substance makes a noticeably different sound when shaken. Tape the lids on firmly. The pots should appear identical in every way; if the labels differ, cover with paper or sticky backed plastic.

Show the child how to mix the cylinders up and then listen to each one by shaking it beside both ears. The aim is to find the pairs through listening and then put them together. If you paint a matching coloured dot on the bottom of each pot, the child can check for herself whether she has matched them correctly.

Later, challenge the child by placing the two sets at opposite ends of the room. The child has to listen to one of the cylinders, remember its sound and hold it in her memory as she crosses the room to listen to the other set and find its match. She then brings it back to check and places the two together if she is correct, or returns it if you want to maintain the level of challenge.

Farmyard sounds

Gather a group of about six children, although you can adapt this game to accommodate more or fewer children. Give each child a farmyard animal to be, for example, a donkey, a chicken, a horse, a cow, a pig and a sheep. Check that they can imitate the noise the animal makes then tell the children a story incorporating all of these animals. The children have to listen carefully and when they hear their animal mentioned, they jump up, make the appropriate sound and sit down again quickly so the story can carry on. The challenge is not to miss your animal. You can have fun trying to catch the children out by referring to the same animal in quick succession, although pick the child carefully if you choose to do this! You can also make the most of the pregnant pause - 'The farmer marched into the farmyard and he put the horse in the stable, the pig

in the pig sty and he noticed that the shed was empty. "Which animal shall I put in the shed?" he thought to himself. "I think I'll put the ...." ' You'll have all your farmyard animals sitting on the edge of their seats waiting to hear who it is to be!

Later, you can develop this game by encouraging the children to choose their own representative noises. Any story can be used as long as it incorporates the right number of characters and an opportunity for each character to be mentioned an equal number of times. Percussion instruments are a useful starting point as they provide a ready-made sound for the children to think about and then apply to a character. Talk about each character before the story begins and discuss with the children what sound would be suitable. For example, the giant could be the drum; the fairy could be the triangle. Encourage them to make suggestions and use their ideas as much as possible.

Sounds all around

Ask your group of children to sit as still and as quiet as they can, and to shut their eyes. Ask them to listen to all the sounds they can hear. To begin with, direct them to focus on certain areas, one at a time: Can they hear sounds their bodies are making? Can they hear sounds in the room? Can they hear sounds from other people in the room? Can they hears sounds from outside? Ask the children to share with the group what they heard when they were listening so carefully (creaking chair, heart beating, tummy rumbling, somebody sniffing, a car). The results could be turned into a group poem:

When I was sitting

As quiet as a mouse

I heard .....

(See 'Watery poems' activity, page 58)

Try doing this in a variety of settings: the back garden, the front garden adjoining the street, perhaps with a group of your older ones near the sandpit where others are playing (it takes a lot of control to keep your eyes closed and listen when you hear lots of activity going on beside you). If you have a settled, older group who are comfortable, offer them blindfolds to help them focus on listening alone - although never try and force the child who is not keen.

Writing letters

Once a child has learned to match a letter with the sound it makes, and her pencil control is sufficient, she can be shown how to write the letter. If you have introduced the child to the symbols for each sound through feely letters and encouraged her to feel the shape of the letter as it is written, she will already have practised controlling her hand to form the correct shape with a writing implement.

What age?

To begin with, the child should be given lots of opportunity to explore making marks with a variety of different resources - in sand, with paint, pencils and other writing implements, in clay and Plasticene, on a blackboard with chalk. As she becomes ready, you can then introduce a number of activities that lead towards the final stage of writing a letter on paper with a pencil. Your children may or may not reach this stage before they leave your setting, but any mark making experience will contribute to the Early Learning Goal requiring children to 'form recognisable letters' by the time they reach the end of their reception year. They also meet the Welsh Desirable Outcome that the child should 'enjoy

marking and basic writing experiences' and the Scottish Curriculum Framework advice that children should 'use written marks...' and 'experiment with symbols (and) letters'.

Writing letters in a sand tray

You need a small tray or the lid of a biscuit tin and enough fine, dry sand to cover the base of the tray. Show the child how to make writing related patterns in the sand - loops, circles, semi-circles, zig-zags, crosses. Show her how to shake the tray gently so she can make a new pattern. Leave her to explore.

At a later stage, offer the child a selection of the feely letters that you know she can feel well. Ask her to choose one, feel it and then show her how to write the letter in the sand using your index and middle fingers. Study the result for a moment or two, then shake the tray gently to remove the letter. Ask her to have a turn. If you have more than one tray, you can do this activity with a small group.

If the prospect of numerous sand trays in your setting unnerves you, do this activity outside or even in or around the sand pit.

Allow the children to explore and play freely with their sand trays. Any mark-making activity is a useful preparation for writing and the child needs to have opportunities to experiment and enjoy marks and symbols, as well as gradually learn to write the 26 letters of the alphabet.

Finger painting letters

Finger painting is a wonderful medium for practising letter shapes. Cover an area of paper so that it is thick with paint and then encourage the child to play with writing related patterns. Later, you can show her how to write the letter shapes with her index and middle fingers. Suggest letters the child knows well and can remember (if she uses feely letters as a guide, they will get covered in paint!) If you are able to keep your letters on constant display, the child can look as a reminder.

Allow the children also to explore and play freely with making marks and symbols in the paint.

Writing in the air

In some ways, this is the most challenging of the lead-up activities to writing on paper in that the child must internalise the letter shape before she can write it in the air. Unlike the other activities, she is not leaving a visual image to refer to as she goes through the writing process.

Simply show the child how to write a letter in the air in front of you. For this activity, it is a good idea to allow the child to trace the feely letter first, to

loops

semi-circles

circles

zig-zags

give her a little reminder of its shape and the movements she will need to make in order to write it.

Writing letters on a blackboard

This activity takes the child closer to writing with a pencil on paper. Use a small blackboard that can be put flat on the table top, rather than an easel style, as this places the child in the most natural position for writing. You also need chubby chalk, preferably in different colours. Try to ensure that the child is in a good writing position - sitting with feet placed on the ground, table not too high so that the child can look down and bear down on her work. Choose letters that she knows and can feel well. Encourage her to feel a letter, then show her how to write it on the blackboard. She can write it as many times as she wishes and then rub out anything she doesn't like.

The advantages of a blackboard stage include the option of rubbing out mistakes and the fact that the chubby chalk is easy to hold and the blackboard grips the chalk so that the writing implement is easier to control. Young children also love to work on blackboards - the sound, tactile feel and black/white contrast is immensely satisfying. Do check that your little blackboards have good surfaces. Some are shiny and difficult to write on. If

you cannot find good quality surfaces, buy blackboard paint from a DIY shop and paint your own.

Writing letters on paper

The final stage is writing letters onto plain white paper. If the child has explored the previous activities, she shouldn't find this stage too difficult. The procedure is the same as the blackboard only this time using paper and pencil. Encourage the child to have several attempts.

There is no need to worry if the child is producing large letters. After a while, you can gently encourage her to make them smaller but at this early stage she needs to focus on shape rather than size.

Recording

You can record the letters the child has written in the same way as you record those letters they have learned to associate with their sounds. Have a little booklet for each child so that she can circle those letters she has worked with. You can then add some kind of mark when you feel the child has mastered writing the letter. You could use the same booklet as the letter sounds and circle with a different colour code or use a different mark - a red circle shows the child has associated sound and symbol, a blue circle or square shows they have written the letter. Alternatively, you could use the same booklet but have two sets of letters for recording sounds and writing. Or you could have two identical booklets but with different covers, one for sound association and one for writing.

Pencil grip

The issue of pencil grip can be controversial. Many people feel that a classically correct grip should not be pursued at all costs. The ultimate aim is to be able to write efficiently, legibly and with a reasonable degree of neatness, and this can be achieved with

a number of different grips. An unusual grip is only worth addressing if it is obviously hampering the child's progress. If you are in a nursery or pre-school and you are in doubt, liaise with the infant schools your children move on to. Whatever your own views, it is not helpful to the child if you begin writing with a liberal approach to pencil grip, only to find that the reception and Key Stage 1 teachers make a big issue of it. The younger you start, the easier it is to encourage at least a 'good enough' grip.

Assessment

Look out for whether the child starts at the top of the letter and how accurately she can form its shape. Make sure that she has retained the ability to write a letter over a period of time before recording that she knows it.

Look out for the child's ability to hold the mark maker effectively. If the child can control the pencil successfully, it does not matter that her grip is not traditional (check the policy of the school your children go on to to ensure your approach doesn't clash.)

What you need:

Writing letters on a blackboard

Small, good quality blackboards

Chubby chalk in a variety of colours

Blackboard rubber or cloth

The feely letters

Apron

Books

Don't Forget to Write Martina Selway (Red Fox) ISBN 0 09 920681 1

What Can I Write? Martina Selway (Red Fox) ISBN 0 09 921372 9

Dear Daddy Philippe Dupasquier (Puffin) ISBN 9 780140 505405

Mice Can't Write Mike and Maria Gordon (Wayland) ISBN 0 7502 2485 1

I can read!

Through games and activities, you can introduce two of the literacy skills that contribute to the child's development as a whole reader:

❏ The use of phonic knowledge to decode words.

❏ Learning commonly used words that are not phonetic and have to be recognised by sight.

What age?

Try the following activities once your child can recognise and associate all the sounds and letters of the alphabet. The age at which the child is ready will vary enormously. Much more important than age is how much general literacy preparation has taken place and how well she can associate letters and sounds. Some children are more than ready during the early years, others may not be ready before they leave your setting.

The Early Learning Goal relating to these activities states that most children should be able to 'read a range of familiar and common words and simple sentences independently' by the end of their reception year. The Scottish Curriculum Framework advice suggests that children should be learning to 'recognise some familiar words' during their pre-school years. If early years practitioners are to meet these goals, it is useful to have some specific reading activities available for children towards the end of pre-school and during reception.

The object game

Gather some familiar objects with short, phonetic names such as lid, hat, dog, pig, pot, mug, hen, box. Set the objects out on the table and discuss them with the child, checking that she knows the names. If you have objects with more than one possible name, try to establish which name you are going to use for this game (for example, hen rather than chicken).

Explain to the child that you are thinking of one of the objects and ask her to guess which one. If the child makes a guess, tell her that whatever it is she has guessed is not the one you were thinking of and that you will give her a clue.

Write the name of one of the objects on a strip of paper, for example 'hat'. Cut the name from the strip and give it to the child. Ask the child to sound out each letter: h-a-t. Encourage her to say the sounds faster and faster until they blend together to form the whole word. She can also have a look at the objects to prompt her in reading and recognising the word.

Ask her to put the written word beside the object and respond positively to the fact that she has read the word.

Repeat the activity for a different object and continue for as long as she is interested. When the activity is finished, ask the child to read through all the labels again.

You can do this with a small group, taking turns, but the process with each individual is quite lengthy so the other children in the group will have to be patient. It is preferable to introduce the activity to individuals if possible and then encourage a group of children to read and match ready prepared labels with the same objects as a shared follow-up activity. If the activity takes off, prepare a box containing suitable objects, along with ready prepared cards. The objects can be changed from time to time to maintain interest.

Don't feel you have to stick to three-letter words. For example, lemon is a more or less phonetic word and with the context of the object, the child should be able to cope with it. If you have introduced some common digraphs to your children such as th, sh, and ai, you can include appropriate objects such as train or ship. It helps the child if you indicate that these two letter sounds go together by putting a little line under them when you write the word or prepare the card - for example, tr<u>ai</u>n or <u>sh</u>ip.

If you write the word in front of the child, it shows the child the link between the two processes of reading and writing; you write your thought and the child reads it.

Puzzle words

Some of the most common words in the English language are not phonetic, which means they cannot be sounded out. The reader has to be able to recognise them by sight. The more access and exposure the child has to books and print in all its forms, the more opportunity she will have to build up a sight vocabulary of these words. As part of leading the child towards whole reading, we can introduce some of these words to the children through games.

What you need:

Puzzle words

Sets of cards with common non-phonetic words, for example: the, where, you, me.

Commonly used non-phonetic words include: the, are, we, she, he, you, was, they, by, here, do, was, any, some, my, your. Make up a card for each word. Explain that we call these puzzle words because we cannot sound them out as we did when we were playing the object game. Try sounding out some of the words and then explain to the children that we just have to learn to recognise them in order to read them.

Select three words that contrast in appearance and meaning (in other words, don't go for 'you' and 'your' or 'me' and 'you' in the same trio).

Phase one

Pick one of your three words and tell the children what it says. Encourage them to think of some sentences or phrases that use the word, starting off with one of your own if necessary. This is important. Meaning is essential to reading, so you do need to place these words in context. If a child is not able to do this, she is not yet ready for the activity.

Repeat for the remaining two words. Go through the words a few times, holding them up and saying them.

Phase two

This is the longest phase, where we give the children experience and practice. Place the three words on the table or floor mat and ask a child to 'Give me the word that says *the*' or 'Point to the word that says *you*' or 'Put the word that says *here* in my hand'.

Mix the cards up in between questions. Continue for as long as seems necessary for the children to learn each word. You can make this stage

active if you need to: 'Becky, go and hide the word *here* in the book corner for Sam to find'. If the children's interest wanes pick the activity up again at the phase two stage, either later in the session or another day.

Phase three

This is the phase where we find out whether the child can remember each word. Ask the child questions, without saying the word: 'Becky, what does this word say?' 'Sam, can you read this one?' If the children cannot read the words independently, simply go back to phase two. If one child can't recognise the words, go back to phase two questions with that child but continue phase three questions for the others.

Puzzle word follow-up activities

Plenty of follow-up activity is important in helping the children fix these words in their minds. Keep a record of which words each child has done and encourage them to look for the words in books.

You can also play 'Hunt the word'. Hide those words the children have learned around your setting or garden and then ask each child to search for a word. If they have done a number of words and the game takes off, you can keep sending them off to find another one. Unless your memory is good, keep a list of the hidden words and tick them off as they are found and brought back to you.

Reading games

Some of the vocabulary activities can be developed into reading games. (See naming objects, the action game, the farm game and the 'Where does it go?' game on pages 30-33.)

Labelling your setting

Make a set of cards or write down on slips of paper the names of familiar objects in your setting. These can

range from simple, phonetic words to something more demanding, depending on the age and reading ability of the child. Some possible words include *jug, cup, shelf, peg, table, chair*. The child reads the word on her card and then goes off to place it beside the appropriate object.

Treasure hunt

Plan a hunt where you write out a number of words to guide the child or children to the treasure. For example, give them a slip of paper with the word *jug*. They have to read the word and then go to the jug in which they find a slip saying *mats*. They go to the pile of mats where they find a slip saying *Sam's peg*. They go to Sam's peg where they find a slip saying *book shelf* (you may need to have given *book* as a puzzle word) - and so on, until they find the treasure. A small treat in the form of the treasure adds to the fun of this game.

You could extend the clues to include actions - hop to Sam's peg, jump to the jug, skip to the bookshelf.

What you need::

Treasure hunt

A series of slips with written clues; some 'treasure'.

Assessment

The object game - can the child accurately identify the sound made by each letter in the word and blend the sounds to make a recognisable word (with the help of the objects as a context)?

Puzzle words - phase three of this activity tells you whether the child is able to look at the word and read it. The follow-up activities are important in helping you to assess whether the child has remembered the word over a period of time.

What Learning Looks Like... 51

Making an alphabet

Compiling an alphabet with your children is an enjoyable way of developing, using and consolidating their knowledge of the 26 sounds and symbols, as well as producing something that has a personal meaning. It is an activity that makes a useful contribution to the Early Learning Goal requiring children to 'link sounds to letters, naming and sounding all letters of the alphabet' by the end of their reception year. It also relates to the broader Welsh Desirable Outcome that children should 'understand that written symbols have sound' and the Scottish Curriculum Framework advice that children should 'develop an awareness of letter names and sounds in the context of play experiences.'

You can use whatever theme you wish for your alphabet. The names of the children in your group make a good starting point. A child's name is one of their most familiar words and the special possession of that child. It is often the first written word the child can recognise and write for herself.

The activity

Work through the alphabet, identifying the initial sound/letter for each child's name and putting them into groups. Ask the children to suggest some other names - friends, relations, characters from stories, famous people. If you have children who can recognise the initial sound of a word (see 'I spy with a difference', page 38), challenge them to come up with names for a particular letter. Some letters are quite difficult to cover. There was a King Xerxes, but unfortunately, like all English words

beginning with x, the name does not begin with the phonetic sound of x. If you have enjoyed any of the books illustrated by Quentin Blake, you can borrow his first name for your q section. If necessary, move on to family names and include names from different cultures.

You will probably need to include the digraphs sh, ch and th to cater for the Charlies, Theos and Shaunas. Although we are working with sounds, there are occasions where the spelling and the initial sound of a name won't tally. In these cases, place the name according to spelling. Charlotte is unlikely to be happy about her name going in the sh section when its spelling begins with ch! If you have older children in your group who are starting to learn the common digraphs, you can explain that when we write Charlotte we put a ch but when we say Charlotte it begins with a sh sound.

Aim to have several names beginning with the same letter. It is easier if you are liberal in what you will accept as a name and include pets' names or generic names such as mummy or daddy.

There are various ways of presenting the alphabet:

Making an alphabet frieze

This is a simple frieze to go on the wall, where each letter has a section of paper. Choose different coloured papers for each section and ask the children to write their names on white paper which can then be cut out and stuck onto the background. White

sticky labels are more expensive but they are quicker and easier to use, particularly if you have a lot of children in the group. Encourage all the children to write their names. Even

---

What you need:

Making an alphabet frieze

26 pieces of paper in a variety of colours plus three extra if you are covering the digraphs sh, ch and th.

Plain white paper, scissors and glue or white sticky labels.

Photographs and drawings of the children, their families, friends and pets.

---

some of your newest, youngest children may be able to produce a written version of some sort or other. For those who are unable to produce anything, either write their name for them or, better still, ask any writers in your group to write on the child's behalf. Write out the names for them to copy - it is important that they spell a child's name correctly for work that is going to be displayed. Your emergent writers can also write any names that may not belong to a particular child - Zara, for example, if this is the name you are going to use for z.

Ask for photos from home to stick beside each name, including any pets, family members or friends whose names appear in the alphabet. The children can also draw pictures of themselves, pets, friends and so on, to add or substitute for a photograph.

Use a template or write the appropriate letter in lower and upper case on each section. Write out an explanation of the activity to go on the wall with the frieze, along the lines of: 'We have made an alphabet of names. Can you find your name?' or 'We have made an ABC of names. Look at our families, friends and pets.' Make this writing as beautiful as possible. It is worth ruling guidelines whenever you have to write something for display because the writing will be a model for the children.

Try to leave space for further names and characters to be added as you go along. This is a good way of maintaining interest in the alphabet and building on news. A child might arrive on Monday morning with the news that her friend Tara came to play on Sunday. You can then ask: 'Would you like to add Tara to our names alphabet?'

You could choose a different way of presenting the frieze. A train with a carriage for each letter, or a caterpillar with 26 body segments. Discuss with the children the background they would prefer and include them as much as possible in cutting out the templates for the different parts.

making an alphabet book

Alternatively, make the sections into a large book. The easiest technique is to punch a hole in the top left-hand corner of each page and then tie the pages loosely with a ribbon so that they can be turned over easily. If you can hang the book from a hook on the wall, with a cushion beneath it (preferably in the book corner) you can then encourage the children to take the book down and sit and look at it whenever they want to.

If the activity takes off, make both a frieze and a book, using different themes. Relate your alphabet to the theme that you and your group are

exploring - animals, seasons, games and toys, words and objects to do with water. The 'Our names' theme fits in well with the topic of 'Me/myself'.

what age?

The activity can be done with a range of ages. Younger ones will not be able to produce and identify words to fit in with a specific letter sound, but they can suggest names if you point them in the direction of family and friends. They will also have the benefit of being exposed to identifying the initial sounds of words and grouping them alphabetically. Those who are able to hear and recognise the initial sound in a word can help to arrange the words as well as make suggestions for particular letters. All the children can be involved in cutting, arranging, sticking and drawing when it comes to preparing your alphabet for display.

making a print alphabet

The activity can also be used to explore different forms of print. This activity is suitable for children who can recognise the letters with ease and have the focus and concentration to search for them. Provide your group with pages from magazines, newspapers and printed boxes or packets. Show them how to look for printed letters, cut them out and stick them onto the appropriate page or section to make a letters book or frieze. This is best done as a group activity, allotting just one or two letters to each child or twosome. Limit the search for the children by giving them sections of a magazine page rather than the whole thing and make sure the samples you put out contain plenty of examples of the letter, as well as interesting and contrasting print styles.

If you have a computer, you could show the children some of the different fonts and they could print out letters to add to their collection. You may wish to restrict the letters in some way - even the most enthusiastic group

is unlikely to maintain enough staying power to do the entire alphabet. For example, you could use just the initial letters of the children's names: if your group consists of Eddie, Akmal, Gabrielle, Hannah, Tom and Marco, you have an e page, an a page, a g page and so on. Or you could use the letters that make up the name of your school or playgroup. For the cover of the book, it's a nice idea for the children to make up their own names from different letters.

If the children struggle to cut out the letters, show them how to draw a rough circle around the letter to cut around first. They can then cut the letter out from within the larger shape; this is much easier because the paper piece they are cutting from is smaller and less unwieldy.

Assessment

Your youngest children will simply be giving you the names of family, friends and pets (with some prompting from you). Keep an eye out for how much prompting they need and the range of names they are able to give you.

Look out for how accurately your older ones can group words according to their initial letter sounds and give you words that begin with a particular sound. Remember that the child's previous experience with 'I spy with a difference' and other alphabet/sound games will have a bearing on her abilities.

Making a print alphabet - watch out for how comfortable the child is with different styles of print. Can she recognise a particular letter in spite of the variety of ways in which it is written?

I'm an author!

Making your own book is a fun way of encouraging children to look at books in a new and different light. Literacy in the fullest sense of the word includes becoming familiar with the book as an object - its structure, its layout and how it is put together. The more comfortable the child is with a book, in all its aspects, the more readily she will start to regard it as an integral part of her life.

This activity helps to meet the Welsh Desirable Outcome that the child should 'enjoy books and know how to handle them carefully and appropriately' and the Scottish Curriculum Framework advice that children should learn to 'understand some of the ... layout of books.'

Getting to know books

Start off by discussing 'the book' as an object with the children. Look at all its different parts and elements, encouraging the children to point out any parts they already know. Explain and give the names of new and unfamiliar elements. These could include the front and back covers, the spine, the title, the names of the author and illustrator, the end-papers (the lining on the inside of front and back covers, often beautifully decorated), the gutter (the crease between the left and right hand page), the publisher and the price.

What age?

Take into account the age, level of understanding and experience in your group when choosing what parts to look at. For very young children, you could keep it as simple as book, page, picture and possibly cover. Concentrate more on showing the children how to handle the book - carrying it carefully, lifting it from the shelf, turning the pages and so on. Parts such as end-papers, gutter and spine are quite straightforward for the children to look at and identify while the publisher, author and illustrator are more abstract. Save these for your oldest and most experienced children. The price of the book will also only be meaningful to the children once they have understood that we have to pay money in order to buy something.

Pick appropriate books to illustrate these different elements. If you are planning to make books with your children, you need to bring alive the concepts of author and illustrator as much as possible. Some books have a picture of the author on the back, helping to make his or her identity a reality for the children. Best of all, invite a children's author to talk to the children - although check that it is someone who can communicate well with the pre-school age group.

Constructing a book

When it comes to the construction of the book, start off by looking at how books are put together. Show the children how the pages are joined, that the covers are made from tougher paper or card than the pages, where on the book the title has been written, and so on. Extend this part of the activity for as long as your group are interested. Wherever appropriate,

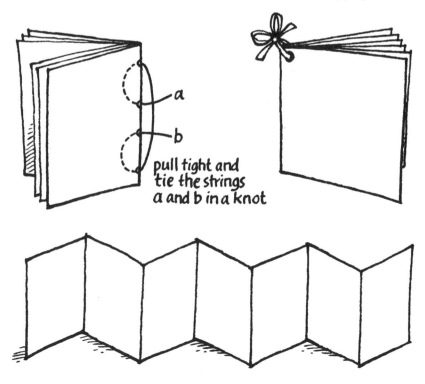

pull tight and tie the strings a and b in a knot

discuss the reasons behind the book's construction, such as why the cover is tougher or why the book's title is written in large, bright letters on the front.

Give the children as much choice as possible in the construction of their book. Begin with the colour of the paper and encourage them to choose a different colour for the book's cover. If you have talked about covers being tougher than pages, you could draw on this by providing thin card. Depending on the degree of choice you are able to cater for, you could also let older children choose the size and shape of their pages. Introduce this idea by looking at different shapes and sizes - small books, large books, square books, long, low rectangular shapes, tall, thin books.

The most authentic construction is to stitch folded paper with a darning needle. This can either be done at the very start so that the children can stick their work onto the ready-made pages, or they can work directly onto the double spreads of paper and these can be stitched together later. The latter technique can raise complications regarding order of information, unless you stick to one side per topic area and don't mind too much about the order in which the pages go.

Other possibilities include punching a hole in the top left-hand corner of each page and tying the pages together with a ribbon, or folding a long piece of paper back and forth to make a zig-zag book. If you have reasonable financial resources and are planning to use a lot of photos or drawings, a small album with clear plastic pockets is another option. You can slip the picture into the left-hand pocket and the accompanying writing into the right-hand pocket. The disadvantage of any pre-constructed book is that the children miss out on the early stages of actually making the book themselves.

If your children are ready, involve them as much as possible with planning the layout of their work. Look at books that have the picture on one page and the writing on the other. Find examples that mix little pictures with the words, and examples of pictures that run across a double-page spread - both the left- and right-hand pages.

You and your children can use any art form for pictures. Picture books are illustrated in a number of different ways. If you have explored lots of art techniques with your children (painting, drawing, print, collage), you can go on to show the children a range of different illustrative styles. For example, you can clearly see the brush strokes in Eric Carle's painted illustrations whereas Ezra Jack Keats uses collage cut from wallpaper and other patterned pieces. Some illustrators use a range of colour, others just two or three and some use only pen and ink drawings. If you wish to extend this project into the Creative Development area, the children could do different types of drawings, paintings, collage and prints to put in their books. Prints are particularly useful for decorating covers or end-papers.

Making a book about the seasons

Making a book enables the children to use and develop their oral language and literacy related skills. It also provides a good format for exploring and presenting work on the seasons because it can easily be divided into four sections. Depending on how much work your children are able to do, this could simply mean four pages, or the book could develop into four chapters. Alternatively, you could do one little booklet for each season so that you end up with a series of four. You can either make a group book or, if you have the time and necessary support, each child can make an

individual book. If you have adults available for individual or small group work, the book can be tailored to fit the child's level of language and literacy development.

A year is a long time in the life of a young child. When looking at the topic of the seasons with the pre-school or reception age-group, you need to concentrate on the 'here and now'. Your children may not remember even the most significant annual events such as Diwali, Christmas or summer holidays. The features and characteristics of each season will make far more sense to them if you carry out your study during the season itself. This does not mean that you cannot refer to the other seasons. For example, when looking at the warm sunny weather in summer you can also talk about the cold, snowy weather in winter - but you do need to tie the main body of the activity to what the child is currently experiencing. This means that a book about all four seasons may take you the entire year to complete.

When it comes to choosing which seasonal aspects to focus on for your book, go for elements that are integral to the young child's life and experience. Seasonal weather and how this affects clothing makes a good choice. The weather impinges directly on the child's daily life, as do the clothes she wears.

Weather through the seasons

A weather chart is a good starting point in helping you and your group to focus on the kind of weather you have been having. You can then go on to establish the broad weather pattern for whichever season you are looking at so that your children are clear that it is generally warm and sunny in summer, or cold and snowy in winter, or misty and getting colder in autumn, or showery and getting warmer in spring.

With your group, gather together words, phrases and sentences to describe the weather. If necessary, lead the children into the discussion by asking them questions such as whether the sun was shining when they arrived and if they felt hot or cold outside at playtime.

You could also give the group a starting point:

'In summer the sun is ...'

'In summer the sky is ...'

'In winter I feel ...'

What you need:

Weather through the seasons

A weather chart

Seasonal pictures, stories. poems

Paper, pen and clipboard for writing down the children's suggestions

Ready constructed book or booklets (for group or individual books)

Art materials for illustrations (coloured pencils, wax crayons, paint, collage materials, printing materials)

Bear in mind that weather is quite an abstract concept. With very young children, focus on elements they will have seen and felt, such as sun, rain, wind, blue skies, grey skies, clouds, mist, snow, hail.

Use pictures, books and poems to help the children think about the seasonal weather and give them ideas for words. This is a favourite topic for children's poets and most anthologies have lots of choices to draw from.

Make a note of the group's suggestions if you are going to make a group book. These suggestions can then be written up later in the form of a list, poem or prose. Any writers in your group can also contribute to this part of the book. If you are going to make individual books, you can follow up the group discussion by sitting down with one or two children to write down their specific thoughts and ideas.

Add appropriate artwork to this part of the book: big yellow suns, blue skies, fluffy white clouds for summer, snowflakes and grey skies for winter. Those children who are not yet able to produce representational work can be given summery or wintry colours to paint or draw with - bright yellow, sky blue and white, or pale greys and pale greens. Use blue and yellow tissue paper and white cotton wool to make summery collages or explore sponge and potato printing to create a sunny sky or a snowy scene.

What age?

You can follow this basic pattern for any age group or ability. Be prepared for the quantity and complexity of the resulting work to vary from child to child, depending on age and developmental level. If you are able to do the activity with just one or two children, you will have more success in encouraging the greatest possible input from the children themselves.

What to wear?

Talking about seasonal weather leads on naturally to seasonal clothing. This works best with summer and winter because they have the most clearly defined weather patterns, although you can also look at waterproof clothing in connection with spring showers.

Show the children photographs or drawings of people wearing appropriate clothing for the seasons - coats, scarves, gloves and wellies in winter, or shorts, T-shirts, sun hats and sandals in summer. Talk about each garment, asking the children if they know the names and naming any that are unfamiliar. You can then follow on with various drawing and labelling activities, geared towards the age and developmental level of your group.

What age?

With your youngest children, concentrate on the oral, naming element of the activity. Give each child a drawing of a person and some cut-out pictures of hats, gloves and scarves. Show them how to stick the cut-outs onto their pictures, using either Blu-tak or glue. If you use glue, it is much easier for little ones to put a blob onto the main picture and then place the cut-out directly on top.

Those children with sufficient skills can draw their own people. They can then attach the cut-out garments to their drawings. You can also write the names of the garments onto sticky labels or slips of paper. Read each label to the child and help her to stick it onto the correct part of the picture.

Your oldest and most advanced children can draw their own hats, gloves and scarves, as well as their own people. For those who are ready, increase the number of garments and introduce some unusual items such as a balaclava helmet or a sun visor. If you have any writers in the group, encourage them to write some or all of their own labels.

The children's work can then be added to the group seasons book or put into their own, individual books.

This activity of labelling a picture is a useful recording technique, helping the child towards the Early Learning Goal of 'attempt(ing) writing for various purposes, using features of different forms ...'

Other seasonal topics

There are a number of topics related to the seasons that you and your children could look at and add to their books:

❏ The seasonal changes in a tree and other plant life.

As each season arrives, observe trees and plants, draw pictures and ask those children who are ready to dictate or write some words explaining their

pictures. Add pressed leaves, autumnal leaves and leaf prints, paintings or sponge prints of spring blossom, drawings of summer fruits and bare winter branches.

Gather and discuss other seasonal plant life - conkers, acorns, nuts, bare winter twigs, evergreen branches, catkins, sticky buds, blossom, horse chestnut candles. Make lists of them for the seasons book. Those children who are ready can observe the nature objects, draw them and label their drawings.

Plant bulbs in autumn and seeds in the spring. Observe, draw and label the results. Sit down with the children to discuss and come up with a set of instructions for planting and looking after a bulb or seed. These can be written down and added to the book.

❏ Seasonal events, such as Christmas, bonfire night, summer holidays, Diwali.

These can be discussed and recorded through words and pictures and added to the book in the appropriate section, according to the season in which the festival or celebration occurs.

❏ The changes in daylight hours, with the nights and days getting longer or shorter depending on the season.

Read Robert Louis Stevenson's poem 'In winter I get up at night ...' from *A Child's Garden of Verses*. You could also explore how the seasons affect the children's play activities, looking at winter games and summer games.

Books

The Book that Jack Made Paul and Emma Rogers (Bodley Head) ISBN 0 370 32306 8 A retelling of Jack and the Beanstalk - and Jack has made this book himself, with smudged paint faithfully reproduced! Includes instructions for making your own book.

Assessment

Getting to know books and **Constructing a book** - look out for the general interest the child shows in 'the book' as an object. What contribution does she make to the actual construction of a book? Does she show an understanding of the different parts through helping to choose the colour of paper, the shape and size of the pages and so on?

Making a book about the seasons - look out for: the level of interest the child shows in the topic; the vocabulary she uses and how well it relates to the topic; the complexity and relevance of her contribution in activities such as describing the weather; how much she can remember of different seasonal weathers and events and how clearly she can describe them. Take into account the child's age, previous experiences, special needs and English as a first or second language when making these assessments.

Some older children may be ready to contribute to the actual writing of the book. If the child's role is to copy, look out for how accurately she is forming the letters and reproducing the words. Depending on her age and previous experience, look out for the size of the letters, how well she is spacing the words and placing them on the page. If she is producing her own content, look out for whether she is able to write common, non-phonetic words such as *the* or *my*, and whether her attempts at writing more complex words are phonetically plausible (see 'From thoughts to symbols', pages 16 and 17.)

Water poems

These activities help the children progress towards a number of the Early Learning Goals, including 'us(ing) language to imagine and recreate .... experiences;' 'us(ing) talk to organise, sequence and clarify thinking, ideas, feelings, events'; 'extend(ing) their vocabulary, exploring the meanings and sounds of new words' and 'attempt(ing) writing for various purposes, using features of different forms ...' They also link with the Scottish Curriculum Framework advice to: 'listen with enjoyment and respond to ... poetry', 'have fun with language' and listen and respond to the sound and rhythm of words ...'

Poetry can follow strict rules of rhyme and metre, but it does not have to follow any rules at all. As long as a poem presents interesting words and ideas and helps you to imagine and think about a subject, you can use whatever form you wish.

This means that poems can be created even by very young children, if they are encouraged to think and talk about a theme or topic. The thoughts, ideas, words, similes and images they come up with as part of an oral activity can be written down by the adult leading the group and then brought together to create a poem. You need no special, poetic skills in order to do this: simply organise the words and phrases in a way that appeals to you and your children.

Organising ideas into poems

One possible approach is to divide the children's ideas into phrases, sentences and single words:

our water is as cold as

an ice cream

and

snow flakes

freezy freezy water!

Even a format as simple as a list of interesting words can work well:

water is

splishy

swishy

splashy

bubbly

gushy

washy

You may find you can put the words and phrases together more or less as they are given to you by the children. Choose a simple starting point and then note down the children's ideas as they come.

making your own water poem

For a poem on the theme of water, a large bowl of water can be used as a trigger for poetic thoughts. If you have a glass or clear plastic bowl, the water will look more beautiful - particularly if it is a sunny day and you position your group near a window or outside so that the water sparkles in the sunlight.

Ask the children to come and swish the water with their hands and think about how it feels. Warm water is soothing in winter, cold water is refreshing on a

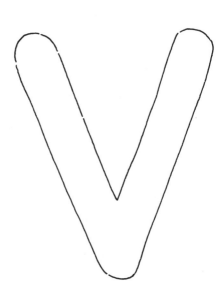

hot day. If your bowl of water is large enough, invite two or even three at a time to minimise the wait for the rest - although you do need to pick your combinations of children carefully.

You can then give your group the first part of the sentence: 'Water feels ....' and ask them to tell you how it felt. Start off yourself if the group needs a little prompting: 'Water feels cool and swishy'. As the children contribute their thoughts, ideas, words and experiences, note them down. If the activity takes off, go on to provide them with something to stir the water and ask them to think about what it looks like. Give each child the first part of the sentence: 'Water is ....' and note down their responses, again starting them off if necessary.

The final stage is to organise their words, sentences and phrases into a poem:

Water is

see-through

and water is wet

water is cold

and bubbly

and sparkly

it is liquid

water water water

By Katie (4.10), Jade (4.6) and Scarlett (5.4)

With poems, you don't need to worry about punctuation!

If you have older children with lots of poetry experience, you may find that you can lead the group towards

What you need:

Making your own water poem

A large, clear plastic bowl filled with warm or cool water

A waterproof mat (if indoors)

Something to stir the water

A hand towel

Paper, pen and clipboard for writing down the children's ideas

Watery backgrounds

At a later stage, the children can create watery backgrounds for displaying the poems. Marbled paper, layers of white and blue tissue with streaks of silver foil; sponge prints in pale blues and white are all great fun to do and give a good watery effect. If you have children who are ready, ask them to write out different parts of the poem to stick onto the watery background.

When it rains ...

Go on to explore other possibilities. Wait for a rainy day and then discuss with the children their experiences of the rain. What did they wear? What did the rain look like, feel like, sound like? What games do they play in the rain? (splashing in puddles, catching raindrops, watching raindrops slide down the window) Read some rainy poems to the children.

You can then give each child the beginning of the sentence - 'When it rains I ....' - and ask them to complete the sentence. Write down

helping you organise the words, phrases and sentences. Read the poem back to the children and explore moving words and phrases about to see which effect works the best.

their responses. Later, gather the sentences into groups of three:

When it rains I splash in the puddles.

When it rains I wear my boots.

When it rains I get all wet.

If you wish, you can make subtle changes to introduce rhythm, for example: 'When it rains I get all wet' fits into the rhythm better than 'When it rains I get wet.'

Read each poem to the group and ask for suggestions to finish the poem off. Try out each ending and together find the one you like best. For example, 'I like rain' or 'It's raining today' or 'Splishy splashy rain':

(1) When it rains I splash in the puddles

When it rains I wear my boots

When it rains I get all wet

I like rain (?)

(2) When it rains I splash in the puddles

When it rains I wear my boots

When it rains I get all wet

It's raining today (?)

Displaying your poems

Again, these can be written out either by the adult or the children and mounted on watery or rainy backgrounds - add raindrops to the watery backgrounds suggested above. The poems can either be put on the wall for everyone to look at and read, or made into a group anthology. (See page 54, 'I'm an author', for ways of constructing a book.) Make sure you attribute the poems to each of the poets who contributed ('A rainy day poem by Jamie, Lara, Kumar and

Dean') and then read regularly to the children from their poetry book as part of their poetry experience.

Poetic tricks

As your poetry writing develops, be on the look-out for poetry that happens spontaneously; for example, alliteration, where several words begin with the same sound. Explain to the children that poems often use words that begin with the same sound - bearing in mind that this will only be meaningful to them if they are able to recognise the initial sounds in words. You could also read some poems that use alliteration and make sure that alliterative words are placed together when the poem is actually compiled from the children's suggestions:

Splish splash splosh

and a little little gosh

paddling

splittering

splattering

By Katie (4.10), Scarlett (5.4) and Ayesha (5.1)

Repetition is another useful poetic trick, and great fun:

Rain is

wet

wet

wet

Similes

Similes are a good source of poetic ideas if your children are ready for them. Whenever possible, seize the moment so that they can draw on real life experiences - for example, getting caught in that shower of rain at playtime. Give them some starting points such as 'This rain is as cold as ...', 'These raindrops are as big a s...', 'These puddles are as splashy as ...' If they get the idea, go on to build their suggestions into a poem:

Our water is as cold as

a freezer

as winter

as wind

as fish

as ice

as a fridge

bubbly bubbly bubbles

By Lara (5.4), Katie (4.10) and Jade (4.6)

Although these activities do not need you or your group to produce rhyme or rhythm, the children may bring these techniques into their poems, particularly if you share lots of poetry with them and play with rhymes and jingles (see 'I spy with a difference', page 38). Give them the freedom to explore rhythm and rhyme - the results can be great fun and inventive:

splish splash splosh

and a little little gosh

paddling

splittering

splattering

it splitters like a splotter

I wish I was an otter

By Katie (4.10), Ayesha (5.1) and Scarlett (5.4)

The more poems you read and the more group poetry writing you can do with your children, the more adept they will become. Keep the group small so that all the children can join in and try to include at least one of your more verbal, imaginative children in each group to help inspire the rest and keep ideas flowing.

Tape recording

Instead of writing, you could record the session. Explain to the children what you are doing and play back the recording so they can hear the ideas they came up with in an oral form. You can then transcribe the tape recording at a later date. Tape recording enables you to keep your attention with the group all the time instead of taking moments out to scribe the children's ideas - useful if you have either a lively group or one which needs lots of encouragement and leading.

Although all the examples given above follow the theme of 'Water', the ideas can be adapted to any theme or even just a one-off activity. Be constantly on the look-out for poems you can borrow from and adapt. And if the children's ideas don't fit together with quite the same degree of rhythm and rhyme as the original inspiration, it doesn't matter a bit as long as everyone has enjoyed themselves!

Assessment

Look out for the range of words and poetic phrases the child gives you. How imaginative is her contribution and does it link with the theme? Depending on the child's age and previous experiences of sound / rhyme games and poetry reading, does she introduce rhythm and rhyme? When creating similes, does the image she suggests make sense?

Older children who are starting to write for themselves may spontaneously introduce poetry into their writing. Look out for and encourage such moments if they occur.

Books

Poetry

A Puffin Book of First Poetry edited by June Crebbin (Puffin) ISBN 0 67 088659 9 A collection of traditional and contemporary rhymes and poems, aimed at the four plus age group.

A Very First Poetry Book (ISBN 0 19 916050 3) and *A First Poetry Book* (ISBN 0 19 918112 8 compiled by John Fisher (Oxford University Press). A good range of poems and rhymes, illustrated by different artists. Suitable for the older ones.

Elephants and Emus and Other Animal Rhymes compiled/illustrated by Philippa-Alys Browne (Barefoot Books) ISBN 1 901223 86 8 A beautifully illustrated collection with something for all ages.

The Nursery Collection Shirley Hughes (Walker) ISBN 0 7445 4378 9 A collection of little books on colour, opposites, size, shape, sound and number. Written in poetic rhyming text.

The colour table

The colour table is a favourite activity when looking at and learning about colours. Choose one or two colours a time and ask the children to find objects to display. If you want the children to bring objects from home, it is worth sending a quick note to parents or mentioning it when they collect their children - particularly with your younger ones.

When you set up your table or shelf, make sure that you cover it with an appropriately coloured cloth. For example, dark blue provides a good foil for yellow or white objects, whereas you would need something light and bright in colour when it comes to displaying black or brown objects.

What age?

With your very youngest children, the colour table simply helps them learn to recognise and name the colours. Talk to them about the objects they have brought in and show them the other objects on the table so that they can start to see the similarity in colour. For older ones, the activity can be developed, giving them the opportunity to see that there are many different kinds of blue, or red or green ... A navy blue crayon is different from the blue of the sky, which is different from turquoise, even though they all come within the broad colour category of blue.

Colour names

Once your children start to recognise the variations in colour, you can draw on their interest in words by developing the language possibilities in your colour table.

Different blues have different names - royal blue, navy blue, sky blue, eggshell blue. Colour comes in different shades - from light or pale blue to dark blue.

Write labels for your different blues and group the objects according to their closest category so that you have all the navy blue things separate from the eggshell blue things. Avoid having too many categories or types of colour that are too similar. For example, pillar box red and bright red are very close, although you can certainly talk to the children about the different names for a colour tone or type. Remember also that this is not an exact science. While you want to avoid putting a pale blue

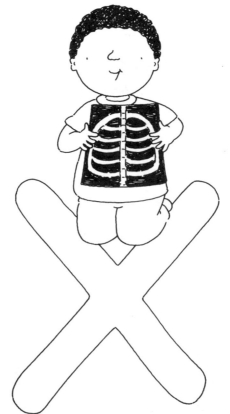

pencil in your navy blue group, it really doesn't matter if the darker blue felt-tip ends up in the royal blue or navy blue part of the table. The aim is to get children thinking about and enjoying colour and its different names.

If your children are ready, talk to them about the origin of some of the colour names. For example, show them a picture of a blackbird's egg and a naval seaman, and talk about how these objects have given their names to eggshell blue and navy blue. With obvious colours, such as sky blue or lemon yellow, ask them to make the link themselves. Hold up a pale yellow cardigan and ask the children: 'Why do you think the colour of this cardigan is called lemon yellow?'

Encourage the children to use these new colour names. On a one-to-one basis, talk about the type of blue the child has used in her painting or drawing. If your children take the colour names and types on board, dispatch them around the room or the garden looking for something navy blue, or pale blue (plant plenty of objects in the room so that the search is not too challenging). If the child brings back something that is a strikingly different colour, try and help her to match it with the closest group of blue objects on the colour table.

Colour similes and poems

Develop the activity into a simile-based poem (see 'Water poems', page 58). Ask each child to choose an object, for example, a yellow teddy. The starting point for the poem is:

What you need:

The colour table

A table or shelf with an appropriately coloured cloth.

Folded cards for writing the names of the different colours.

Colour poems

Some coloured objects such as a yellow teddy, a green apple, a red balloon.

Paper, pen and clip board for writing down the children's suggestions.

Paint, including white and black to mix the appropriate shades to decorate the poems.

Paper, glue, scissors for making book or frieze to display poems.

My teddy is as yellow as ...

The child can then use objects from the colour table for inspiration, or think up new possibilities. Take dictation from each child so that you can make a collection of colour poems:

My teddy is as yellow as a

lemon

or a primrose

or yellow paint

or a piece of cheese

My apple is as red as a

red balloon and a

letter box and a

red felt-pen and

my mummy's lipstick

Your poems could also focus on a specific shade, again using a simile format. As part of your work on the theme of 'Colour', try to cover a range of shades and types with different children to create a set of poems all about one colour:

My jumper is navy blue like a sailor

like teddy's eyes

like my socks

My car is sky blue like the sky

like a forget-me-not

like Hannah's hair-band

Each poem can be then decorated with paint mixed to the shade of blue used in the poem and turned into a book or a frieze for the wall.

Common colour names

Blue: navy, royal, sky, eggshell, turquoise.

Red: scarlet, crimson, pillar box, ruby, cherry.

Yellow: lemon, mustard, gold, amber, ochre.

Green: leaf, emerald, sea, khaki, bottle.

Assessment

With your youngest children, you need to assess whether the child can recognise and correctly name the colour of an object. Finding objects of a given colour for the colour table is one indication that the child has acquired this knowledge. Aim for your children to be able to recognise and name red, blue and yellow, green, orange and purple, brown, grey, pink and black and white by the time they leave your setting.

With older ones, look out for the degree of interest they show in other colour names and whether they remember them. Are they able to work out why a colour is given a particular name (such as lemon yellow)? When grouping objects into colour types and making colour simile poems, are they (within reason) able to identify the particular colour type of an object?

Talking pictures

The theme of 'All about me' is appropriate because it focuses on a familiar topic. The young child of today has a busy life and an eventful past. You can use oral language, pictures and writing skills to help her focus on and record details about herself, her family and events from both present and past. This makes the activity particularly relevant to the Early Learning Goal of 'us(ing) talk to organise, sequence and clarify thinking, ideas, feelings and events'.

Using photographs

Speak directly to parents or send a note home requesting that the child bring in photographs of herself at different ages Ask for at least three, but no more than six. If possible, the photographs should contrast in age. For example, a new-born baby photo, a crawling or toddling photo and a second or third birthday party.

Talk about each photograph with the child. Encourage her to tell you about herself and the picture - what she is wearing, what she is doing, who else is in the photo, and so on. Talk about the age of the child in the photograph compared with her current age. As much as possible, allow her to take the conversational lead.

Explain that you and she are going to stick her photograph onto a piece of paper. With your older ones, begin by explaining that you are going to write down what they want to say about their photos for

other people to read. If you feel it is necessary, show her another child's picture and sentence, to help her realise the purpose of the activity. Say to her: 'This is what Tom wanted to say about his photograph', point to the words and then read them.

Prompt her with suggestions if necessary and write one or two sentences, keeping as close to her words as possible:

My name is Katie. I am 4 years old. I have a pretty face. I am good at drawing. *(Katie 4.10)*

My name is Joanne. I am very special.

Katie and Scarlett are my best friends. Katie helps me when I fall over.

(Joanne 4.5)

Read back what you have written. If the child is ready to assess what has been recorded, see if there is anything she would like to change or add.

What age?

This activity is suitable for all ages in the early years setting. One of the Welsh Desirable Learning Outcomes suggests that children should be able to 'identify and explain events illustrated in pictures' - something you can start working towards from a very young age. Make the most of the photographs as an opportunity to chat to and link with your youngest, newest children. With the younger ones (and some older ones) you will be selecting and writing down information rather than taking dictation. You could also ask parents to do this at home with their child. Parental input of this kind is particularly helpful with very little ones or children with special needs. Mum, dad and older siblings usually understand the child's speech better than other adults and the quiet child is much more likely to open up at home. Ask parents to send in their transcripts for you to copy out later. If parents are anxious about 'getting it right', reassure them that the main value of the activity is to chat freely about the photo. The writing does not have to be word for word or follow any particular format, as long as it approximates to the child's own thoughts.

If you have children whose home language is not English, ask the parent to write the words for you and provide a translation, so that you can include both versions on the child's picture. This is a useful way of helping bilingual children to link their two languages, as well as introducing the concept of 'other languages' to the rest of your group.

Discuss and write about as many of the photographs as your child has the interest for. If you manage more than one, or if home provides more, sit down with the child and talk about the order in which they should go At this point, you are developing the 'All about me' information into a kind of story because you are using the story technique of a *sequence* of events. The success of this part of the activity will depend on the child's ability to put events into their order of occurrence, something most children in the early years setting should be able to manage with a little prompting and support from an adult.

making a display

Make a display of the children's photographs and words. Choose brightly coloured background paper and involve the children in the cutting and sticking as much as possible. For those children who have been able to put their photographs into order, you can turn their work into a story line.

Have a long strip of paper or attach the separate sheets of paper, one on top of the other, so that the baby photograph and related words are at the top and the most recent photo at the bottom. If you are doing this with

children of five or six (and possibly four-year-olds), signify in some way that each piece of paper or segment represents a year in the child's life. Write the number of each year on the section: '1 year old' at the bottom of the first; '2 years old' at the bottom of the second, and so on.

If you have an older child with a good grasp of the concept of time, you can

show her where to stick each picture in relation to her age in the photograph. For example, the new born photograph would go at the top of the first section representing her first year. The photo of her standing holding on to the table would go at the bottom of the first section, signifying that she was nearly one. The photo of her third birthday would go at the top of the third section, the photo of her on holiday when she was nearly four would go at the bottom, and so on.

Each story line can then be entitled: 'Hannah's story line' with the child's date of birth added underneath.

Encourage the children to include their own drawings and decorate their story lines with stickers, prints, patterns or collage. Although you have done

the writing and overseen the assembling of the work, this needs to be as much the child's own creation as possible. This is a labour intensive activity for the adult. It has to be done either on a one-to-one or in a very small group (another reason for encouraging parents to do the talking and writing at home!).

(For information about the dictation technique see 'Dictation' on page 36.)

Assessment

How articulate is the child in talking about her picture, taking into account age, previous experiences, special needs and whether English is a first or second language? To what extent can she lead the conversation, or is she completely reliant on prompting from you? Do her words and comments link with the picture? If you are putting three photographs in order, how much of a part can she play in sequencing them for herself?

Some older children may be able to write or contribute to writing about their photos. If the child's role is to copy, look out for how accurately she is forming the letters and reproducing the words. Depending on her age and previous experience, look out for the size of the letters and how well she is positioning the words on the page (spaces between words and keeping writing horizontal for example.) If she is producing her own content, look out for whether she is able to write common, non-phonetic words such as *the* or *my,* and whether her attempts at writing more complex words are phonetically plausible (see 'From thoughts to symbols', pages 16 and 17).

Role play activities

Role play is an active and open-ended means of enabling the young child to explore her experiences, develop an understanding of the world around her and externalise her inner thoughts. Children 'make believe' all the time in their spontaneous play. Pretending comes naturally to the young child and makes up an extremely important part of her development. You can build on these natural tendencies by using role play activities as a part of looking at and exploring a theme or topic.

Role play helps the children progress towards a number of the Early Learning Goals. It relates in particular to 'us(ing) language to imagine and recreate roles and experiences'. Other relevant goals include 'using talk to organise, sequence and clarify thinking, ideas, feelings and events' and 'interact with others, negotiating ... activities and taking turns in conversations'.

Role play lends itself particularly well to the theme of 'People who help us'. The wide group of people who fall into this category tend to have clearly defined and recognisable roles. Together, they offer something to suit all interests and temperaments. Many of the roles also involve interaction with the children. For example, when the child visits the doctor, she is participating as a patient in real life and witnessing at first hand the role of the doctor in treating her.

The starting point

Although you should let the children give free rein to their imaginations, they do need a basis of real experience to use as a platform for their dramatic exploration. If you are going to ask a young child to put herself in someone else's shoes, it is essential that she has

something to draw from. The best starting point is a recent, first-hand experience. As part of your topic planning, invite adults into your setting to talk to the children about their jobs. As much as possible, choose people whose roles hold some meaning for the child - your accountant may be helpful but his or her job is not particularly relevant to your group! On the other

hand, the school gardener is probably a familiar figure already and his or her work has direct and noticeable effects on the children. Some other possibilities include:

❑ the community police officer

❑ the school nurse for your area

❑ the lollipop lady (school crossing patrol person)

❑ a childminder or nanny

❑ a swimming pool attendant

❑ the school cleaner or caretaker

❑ a bus driver, train driver, taxi-driver or pilot

Many companies or organisations have community affairs or school liaison personnel who will arrange for someone to visit your school. Don't forget to ask parents - it's a good opportunity to involve fathers, and remember that some mothers may be taking a career break from an appropriate job (teachers, dentists, doctors, shop-workers, librarians, nurses). Retired grandparents may also be willing to come and talk to the children.

If you invite a professional into your setting, check that they are happy (and able) to speak to the pre-school age group and encourage them to bring in equipment to make the session as visual as possible. If a parent or grandparent comes in, discuss with them the kind of information to include and the level at which to pitch their talk.

Better still, visit the work place itself. This is even more useful in giving children first-hand experiences. For example, a trip to the library shows the children where and how the librarian does her work. Taking a walk to the lollipop lady's crossing point and experiencing the way in which she guides pedestrians across the road will mean much more than an explanation.

Planning the activity

Following a visit to or from a 'person who helps us', choose some element of their job that particularly interested the children. Think through which aspects of the role would be feasible for your children to act out and make a note of the words and phrases that were used so that you can prompt the children if necessary.

You also need to gather together any relevant props, costumes or equipment. In the beginning, choose a simple activity with a clear and limited sequence of events. As your children become more experienced at group role play, you can be more ambitious in the situations and dramatic roles you set up.

Beginning the activity

The lollipop lady is a simple, straightforward scenario to begin with. Talk to the children about their visit. Establish what they can remember and go through the sequence of events with them, putting them into order. Remind yourselves of what was said - in this case, thanking the lollipop lady as you walk past and the lollipop lady's response. Talk about why we have lollipop ladies and the particular way in which they help us. Link your discussion with any other experiences the children may have had. Some may use the lollipop lady regularly when

walking to 'big school' with mum and an older sibling. Others may have come across a lollipop lady in stories or television programmes and adverts.

Provide simple props - a lollipop (paint a disc of card and tape to a stick); a white coat (adapt an old white shirt or T shirt) and a cap; cut out cardboard steering wheels for the car drivers and provide hats and scarves for the pedestrians.

Assign roles to the children. To begin with, your lollipop lady (or man) needs to be a child who is comfortable with performing, as well as having a clear grasp of what the role involves. Choose some children to be car drivers. The rest of the group can be the pedestrians. If necessary, take one of the parts yourself to get things started. As the children settle into the activity, you can withdraw and leave them to develop the role play for themselves.

Keep the activity going for as long as it holds the children's interest. Try to ensure that every child is offered the chance to play each role. For this reason, it is often easier to keep the

group small or repeat the activity the next day. As long as the children are enjoying themselves, they gain enormously from repetition.

Be open-minded and flexible as to how the children develop their little drama. While the lollipop lady takes central stage, the pedestrians and car drivers also have their roles to play. The children may extend this part of the activity by drawing on their own experiences of walking to school with a parent and siblings, or driving in the car. Sit back and watch as the children become fussy, impatient or kind mums and dads; naughty or well behaved little pedestrians. Some children may want to be dogs or cats. Your road users may prefer to drive buses or lorries and will probably embellish their roles with appropriate sound effects!

Be flexible, but keep in mind the key points you want your children to draw from the activity. For example, you do want to emphasise that the lollipop lady provides a safe crossing place for adults and children. You may also want to emphasise that pedestrians should thank the lollipop lady as they pass - a good opportunity to reinforce the social technique of giving and receiving thanks.

What age?

The flexible nature of this activity makes it ideal for a group made up of mixed ages and developmental levels. Older and more verbal children can be encouraged to use lots of language. Those who find it difficult to sit still can be helped to introduce lots of movement. You can adjust the amount of guidance you give to support your younger children or children with special

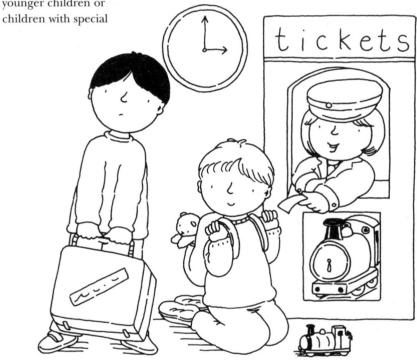

needs, withdrawing as they grow more confident. You can also choose roles carefully to suit the needs of each child.

If you have older children who can guide younger ones, try to organise the roles accordingly. For example, in the lollipop lady activity, the older child playing the parent can take the lead for the younger ones. Alternatively, you can ask a helper to join in. If children are not ready to take a central role, offer them the chance to try on the costumes and hold or use the props. If

a child does not want to join in at all, encourage her to sit and watch. Little ones are often fascinated by watching older children at play and they can absorb all kinds of useful information about language, movement and behaviour through this observation.

Try to choose roles that reflect the experience of your particular group. This will vary, depending on the location of your setting. For example, children are less likely to walk to school in some rural areas and a figure such as the lollipop lady will be

meaningless to them. They may, however, rely more on the bus service - in which case you could plan a role-play session around the bus driver.

In a similar way, try to reflect the different cultural backgrounds of the children in your setting. If you have a mixed race group, ask parents to suggest roles to reflect their particular cultural identity. This has the two-fold benefit of enabling some children to explore their home culture and introducing new cultural experiences to others.

What next?

Once you have finished your role play, it is important to make the clothes and props available to the children so that they can follow up the activity whenever they want to. Group role play is inevitably limited by time. It is also an activity conducted, and to a large extent controlled by the adult. To gain the fullest possible benefits, the children should be given the opportunity to explore the situation independently, if they wish to. When this occurs, do take a few minutes to observe the children (preferably without them realising). These observations will tell you a lot about the child's language skills, use of imagination, knowledge and understanding of the topic you have been looking at.

Assessment

When assessing the child's performance in role play, always take into account age, previous experiences, any special needs and whether English is the child's first language.

Look out for how confidently the child performs, whether or not she can remember and use appropriate vocabulary and phrases and how she extends and develops her role. How well does her body language and speech express the role she is playing? How well is she able to share the stage with others: for example, interacting with other children and waiting quietly while someone else plays their part?

Enabling the children to use the clothes and props independently at a later stage gives you the opportunity to observe whether the child performs differently in a more informal, play situation.

Language and **Literacy**

Planning and the Early Learning Goals

Most of the work done in an early years setting is truly cross curricular. When a child is sitting and listening to a story not only are they developing their language and listening skills they are developing their personal, social and emotional skills as well.

But early years practitioners are obliged to work towards the Early Learning Goals - and their equivalent in other areas of the United Kingdom - so the following three pages will help you plan which goals you are aiming for and help you list them when you plan your work.

The information here is based on the English document but it is still valuable as a guide for other UK countries.

English Early Learning Goals for Language and Literacy

Speaking and listening

S1- enjoy listening to and using spoken and written language, and readily turn to it in their play and learning

S2 - explore and experiment with sounds, words and texts

S3 - listen with enjoyment and respond to stories, songs and other music, rhymes and poems and make up their own stories, songs, rhymes and poems

S4 - use language to imagine and recreate roles and experiences

S5 - use talk to organise, sequence and clarify thinking, ideas, feelings and events

S6 - sustain attentive listening, responding to what they have heard by relevant comments, questions or actions

S7 - interact with others, negotiating plans and activities and taking turns in conversation

S8 - extend their vocabulary, exploring the meanings and sounds of new words

S9 - retell narratives in the correct sequence, drawing on the language patterns of stories

S10 - speak clearly and audibly with confidence and control and show awareness of the listener, for example by their use of conventions such as greetings, 'please' and 'thank you'

Reading

R1 - hear and say initial and final sounds in words, and short vowel sounds within words

R2 - link sounds to letters, naming and sounding the letters of the alphabet

R3 - read a range of familiar and common words and simple sentences independently

R4 - know that print carries meaning and, in English, is read from left to right and top to bottom

R5 - show an understanding of the elements of stories, such as main character, sequence of events, and openings, and how information can be found in non-fiction texts to answer questions about where, who, why and how

Writing

W1 - use a pencil and hold it effectively to form recognisable letters, most of which are correctly formed

W2 - use their phonic knowledge to write simple regular words and make phonetically plausible attempts at more complex words

W3 - write their own names and other things such as labels and captions and begin to form simple sentences, sometimes using punctuation

W4 - attempt writing for various purposes, using features of different forms such as lists, stories and instructions

What Learning Looks Like...

Language and **Literacy**

Planning guide

Story time (page 26)

Story time and story related activities help reading development, writing development (content) and listening skills. Any discussion related work helps the development of speaking skills.

Writing goal W4, reading goal R5.

Narrative awareness: The main character - Reading goal R5, speaking goals S5, S6 and S7

Poster making - S8

Story endings - S4, S5, S6, S7, S9.

Word games (page 30)

These games develop oral language, particularly learning new words and exploring the meanings of words. They contribute to the speaking goal S8.

As reading activities they contribute to R3.

Naming objects can also be carried out as a simple writing activity, contributing to the writing goals W2 and W3.

The action games contribute to S3.

The farm game also contributes to speaking goals S5 and S7 (through the conversation that takes place during the activity).

News time (page 34)

This activity helps both speaking and listening skills. It can also help the early stages of writing in terms of content - thinking about what to say and how to express your thoughts in words.

Speaking and listening goals S4, S5, S6, S9, S10

I spy with a difference (page 38)

Helps both reading and writing skills through recognition of the sounds that make up spoken language.

Reading goals R1. Also lays foundation for R2 and R3.

Writing goals - Lays foundation for W2 and W3.

Dictation (page 36)

Helps the development of speaking skills. Enables the child to witness and be a part of the writing process and see the link between writing and reading.

Talking about pictures; Written communications - Speaking goals S4, S5. Writing goal W4 (through adult taking dictation).

Themes and topics - The above plus speaking goal S6.

Stories - The above plus S9

Feely letters (page 42)

This activity contributes to both reading and writing in helping the child link sound with its matching symbol. Feeling the letter helps prepare the hand for writing its shape - the activity is a direct preparation for actually writing the letter.

Writing goal W1.

Reading goal R2.

Writing letters (page 48)

Relates to the physical element of writing - exploring mark making and forming letters on a surface with a mark maker.

Writing goal W1.

Listening games (page 46)

These help develop listening skills. They all contribute to the speaking and listening goal S6.

70 What Learning Looks Like...

I can read! (page 50)

Through games and activities two reading skills are introduced and practised - phonic techniques to decode words and learning non-phonetic words by sight.

The object game - Helps reading goal R3.

Puzzle words - Helps reading goal R3.

Reading games - R3.

Seasons: I'm an author! (page 54)

Helps the children to learn about books as physical objects, to find their way around them, develop familiarity and hence become more comfortable with them.

Helps speaking and listening skills through conversation and discussion about the theme, also writing skills (content) through dictation and learning about some of the functions of writing and opportunities to witness the link between reading and writing.

Making a book - Reading goal R5.

Making a book about the seasons - Speaking goals S4, S5, S6, S7.

Writing goals W2, W4 through dictation, and own writing with those who are ready.

Making an alphabet (page 52)

Gives foundations for reading/writing - sound / letter recognition.

Writing goal 2 (own names).

Reading related goal R2.

People who help us: Role play activities (page 66)

Role play activities help the child develop speaking and listening skills. They contribute to most of the speaking and listening goals in particular S4. They also contribute to goals S5, S6, S7, S8 and S10.

The activities can also help reading goal R4, particularly in relation to showing understanding of 'main character' and 'sequence of events'.

Water: Water poems (page 58)

Helps speaking and listening skills through playing with and exploring language. Opportunity to use language poetically; learn new words; explore rhythm and rhyme.

Opportunity to witness a function of writing and the link between reading and writing, through the dictation part of the activity.

Speaking goals S4, S5, S6, S7, S8.

Writing goal W4.

Colour: The colour table (page 62)

Contributes to speaking and listening skills through discussion and learning new words and phrases.

Speaking goals S2 and S8.

All about me: Talking pictures (page 64)

This is a conversation based activity with the children's thoughts and ideas recorded through dictation.

It contributes towards speaking goals S1, S2, S3, S4, S5, S6 S7. Writing goal W4.

Early Learning Goals for Language and Literacy	SPEAKING AND LISTENING										READING					WRITING			
	S1	S2	S3	S4	S5	S6	S7	S8	S9	S10	R1	R2	R3	R4	R5	W1	W2	W3	W4
Story time																			
Word games																			
News time																			
Dictation																			
I spy with a difference																			
Feely letters																			
Listening games																			
Writing letters																			
I can read!																			
Making an alphabet																			
Seasons: I'm An Author!																			
Water: Water poems																			
Colour: The colour table																			
All about me: Talking pictures																			
People who help us: Role play activities																			